GIOVANNI
AND
LUSANNA

Lovers in a courtyard

Giovanni and Lusanna

LOVE
AND MARRIAGE
IN RENAISSANCE
FLORENCE

With a New Preface

GENE BRUCKER

UNIVERSITY
OF CALIFORNIA
PRESS
BERKELEY
LOS ANGELES
LONDON

University of California Press
Berkeley and Los Angeles, California

University of California Press, Ltd.
London, England

Library of Congress Cataloging-in-Publication Data

Brucker, Gene A.
  Giovanni and Lusanna : love and marriage in
  Renaissance Florence : with a new preface /
  Gene Brucker.—[2005 ed.]
      p.   cm.
  Includes bibliographical references and index.
  ISBN 0-520-24495-8 (pbk. : alk. paper)
  1. Adultery—Italy—Florence—Case studies.
  2. Marriage—Italy—Florence—Case studies. 3. Social
  classes—Italy—Florence—Case studies. 4. Social
  history—Medieval, 500–1500—Case studies. 5. Florence
  (Italy)—Social conditions—Case studies. 6. Florence
  (Italy)—History—Sources. 7. Renaissance—Italy—
  Florence.   I. Title.

HQ806.B78 2005   2004058860
306.81'0945'5109024—dc22

14   13   12   11   10   09   08   07   06
10   9   8   7   6   5   4   3   2

CONTENTS

PREFACE TO THE 2005 EDITION

It was a quarter-century ago, in the spring of 1980, when I first encountered in the Florentine archives the fragments of a judicial process before the ecclesiastical court of the archbishop Antoninus. The final result of that initial exposure to a puzzling case was a little book *(libricciuolo), Giovanni and Lusanna,* published by the University of California Press in 1986. In the preface to that edition I wrote that the book belonged to a new genre of microhistory, then in its infancy. Microhistory has become more robust over time, with an expanding field of practitioners and a well-developed theoretical foundation for its methodology. In their introduction to *Microhistory and the Lost Peoples of Europe,* Edward Muir and Guido Ruggiero surveyed the evolution of the genre, with a particular emphasis on its Italian progenitors: Carlo Ginzburg, Giovanni Levi, Carlo Poni, and Edoardo Grendi.[1] They also discussed the criticisms that have been levied against microhistories: that by focusing on atypical, unique events, they cannot illuminate broader historical issues; that they read their biases and prejudices back into the past; and that they misread the evidence.

Echoes of these criticisms occur in the lengthy

review of *Giovanni and Lusanna* by Thomas Kuehn, an authority on Florence's legal system and social structure.[2] Kuehn argues that I was too prone to regard these legal texts as reflecting reality rather than view them as constructs designed to further an agenda. He contends that while these documents can be utilized to write an account of the legal battle between Florentine lovers, they were stitched together by lawyers and notaries for the benefit of their clients and cannot accurately describe the history of Giovanni and Lusanna's relationship. I found much merit in Kuehn's critique of my book. I agree with his contention that more examples of litigation over marriages in Tuscan courts would strengthen the analysis and clarify the degree to which this dispute was either common or atypical. His emphasis on the role of lawyers and notaries in creating the legal dossier is a valid point, and one that I could have given more emphasis to in my account.

Nevertheless I am not persuaded by his argument for imposing interpretive limits on this source. I do not see the need to place the evidence from court record in a privileged category. As historians we have a responsibility to weigh all of the evidence that we use: to consider its value, its validity, its plausibility. There is little neutral or value-free data available to us; we must use our judgment, our sense of the parameters of interpretive possibilities, of what is plausible and what is not. And we must be willing to admit in some cases that we cannot explain an act or an event or a motive. Georges Duby once wrote about marriage in early Capetian society: "And what did what we call love have to do with it all? I must say at once and emphatically that we do not know, and what is more, no one ever will."[3] We will never completely know Lusanna's motives for instigating a lawsuit against Giovanni. We can only hope to gain some glimpses of possibilities, of options, of choices, as we search for meaning in that murky past. In a recent example of such work, Thomas and Elizabeth Cohen have demonstrated how effectively these cases can be exploited to construct a model of mid-sixteenth-century Roman society and its rural environs, in two volumes of trials drawn from voluminous judicial records of Roman courts. Their perceptive commentaries on these courtroom dramas do succeed in "throwing back heavy shutters to open a window on the past."[4]

Since the publication of *Giovanni and Lusanna* in 1986, social historians have greatly expanded our knowledge of Italian marriage practices and problems. Daniele Lombardi has written a comprehensive analysis of marriage in Tuscany from the late fifteenth to the late eighteenth century.[5] A recent compilation of essays by an international coterie of scholars have focused on "the ceremonies and festivities surrounding weddings; law and the intervention in marriage by church and state; intermarriage among social groups; and the consequences of marriage for women."[6] Two important collections of essays sponsored by the University of Trent have focused on failed or contested marriages in the peninsula from the twelfth to the eighteenth century.[7] Joanne Ferraro has written a valuable monograph on marital conflict in Venice from the mid-sixteenth to the mid-seventeenth century.[8] Her foray into the records of Venice's patriarchal court reveals how varied and widespread were the sources of spousal discord: sexual dysfunction, physical maltreatment, dowry disputes, abandonment.

The Italian Renaissance continues to kindle the interest not only of scholars but also of that elusive phenomenon, the general reader. Historical novels of the period—Dan Brown's *The Da Vinci Code,* Sarah Dunant's *The Birth of Venus,* and Lauro Martines's *Loredana: A Venetian Tale*—attract a clientele as substantial as did George Eliot's *Romola* more than a century ago. One critic has suggested that a title invoking "that magical period the Renaissance and linking marriage and war" is guaranteed to appeal to a large audience.[9] It can be argued that the lives of historical figures—Giovanni, Lusanna, and their relatives and neighbors—teach us more about the world of the Italian Renaissance than those of any fictional characters. As my colleague the late Carlo Cipolla once remarked: "Why read novels when history is so much more interesting?"

Berkeley
August 2004

1. (New York, 1991). For a current perspective on microhistory and its "cousin," incident analysis, see R. Darnton, "It Happened One Night," in the *New York Review of Books,* June 24, 2004, p. 61.

2. "Reading Microhistory: The Example of *Giovanni and Lusanna,*" *Journal of Modern History* 61 (1989): 514:34.

3. trans., B. Bray, *The Knight, the Lady, and the Priest* (New York, 1983), p.7.

4. *Words and Deeds in Renaissance Rome: Trials before the Papal Magistrates* (Toronto, 1993); *Love and Death in Renaissance Italy* (Chicago, 2004), p.4.

5. *Matrimoni di antica regime* (Bologna, 2001).

6. Joanne Ferraro's review of T. Dean and K. J. P. Lowe, eds., *Marriage in Italy, 1300–1650* (Cambridge, 1998) in *Renaissance Quarterly* 52 (1999): 865.

7. S. Seidel Menchi and D. Quaglioni, eds., *Coniugi nemici. La separazione in Italia dal XII al XVIII secolo* (Bologna, 2001).

8. *Marriage Wars in Late Renaissance Venice* (Oxford, 2001).

9. Anne Schutte, review of *Marriage Wars in Late Renaissance Venice,* in *Sixteenth Century Journal* 34 (2003): 244.

PREFACE TO THE
FIRST EDITION

In the spring of 1980 I was working in the Florentine state archives, collecting material for a study of the Tuscan church in the fifteenth century. I had begun a systematic reading of the protocols of Florentine notaries who redacted documents for ecclesiastical institutions in the city and dominion. In the surviving records of one notary, Ser Filippo Mazzei, I read some pages of testimony by witnesses who had appeared before the archbishop's court to testify in a judicial process involving an alleged marriage. The shape and substance of the case emerged slowly and fitfully, since the records were scattered randomly through several volumes of Ser Filippo's notarial corpus. As I pieced together the dossier of the case, my interest grew and indeed became obsessive. During my last weeks in the archives I temporarily abandoned my research on the church to concentrate on the story of Giovanni and Lusanna and to search for more clues to their lives and fortunes. A return visit to the archives in 1983 enabled me to fill in some gaps in the account and to write a preliminary draft of this tale of two Florentine lovers.

The story of Giovanni and Lusanna fits into a

genre of historical writing, microhistory, that
has recently achieved some notoriety in the discipline. Seven years ago Lawrence Stone published an article entitled "The Return of Narrative" (*Past and Present*, no. 85 [November 1979]:
3–24). Stone had discerned a revival of interest
among American and western European scholars
in writing history that was "descriptive rather
than analytical and [with] its central focus . . . on
man not circumstances." He suggested that this
trend was inspired at least in part by a growing
disenchantment with the various types of "sci-
entific history" that had become so popular in the
years after World War II. In 1972 the eminent
French historian Emmanuel Le Roy Ladurie had
written an obituary for narrative history: "Pres-
ent-day historiography with its preference for the
quantifiable, the statistical and the structural . . .
has virtually condemned to death the narrative
history of events and the individual biography"
(*The Territory of the Historian*, 111, cited by Stone,
23). But a few years later, in 1979, Le Roy Ladurie
himself published a work of microhistory: the
story of an uprising during Carnival in 1580 in
the French town of Romans. Other noteworthy
examples of the genre that have recently appeared
include Carlo Ginzburg's tale of the Friulian
miller Menocchio (*The Cheese and the Worms*,
1980); Natalie Davis's account of the footloose
peasant Martin Guerre and his impersonator (*The
Trial of Martin Guerre*, 1983); and Judith Brown's
poignant story of the nun Benedetta and her

tribulations in a Tuscan convent (*Immodest Acts*, 1985).

In addition to their employment of the narrative mode of exposition, these microhistories are characterized, first, by an emphasis on particular individuals and events, not on groups or structures; and second, by a predilection for the study of people and milieux hitherto unknown and unexplored. Thus, the subjects of these books are frequently peasants, artisans, vagabonds, common soldiers, witches, prostitutes, nuns, friars, and parish priests from the lower echelons of the social order. By far the richest source for these obscure lives has been the records of courts, both secular and ecclesiastical, which exist in thousands of European and American archives and libraries. From this vast, largely untapped repository of judicial records, the patient and careful researcher can reconstruct particular images of "the world we have lost" and of people who inhabited that world. When successful, this microcosmic focus conveys a sense of immediacy, intimacy, and concreteness that is often absent from analytical histories.

I thank the staffs of the Archivio di Stato, Florence, and the Archivio Segreto Vaticano in Rome for facilitating my research on this book. I am grateful to my friend Dott. Paolo Simoncelli of the University of Rome for his diligent if ultimately unsuccessful search for an elusive papal bull. My Berkeley colleagues Professor John

Noonan and Dr. Steven Horwitz provided me with valuable information on specific points of canon law, as did Dr. Christiane Klapisch-Zuber of the Ecole des Hautes Etudes en Sciences Sociales (Paris) on Florentine marriage customs. To Dorothy Shannon, my gratitude for typing the manuscript in its several versions with exemplary care and patience.

THE CONTEXT

Ser Filippo Mazzei was a Florentine notary whose career spanned the middle decades of the fifteenth century. The record of his professional activities has survived in twenty volumes of notarial protocols housed in the state archives of Florence. Copied in Ser Filippo's neat hand in a formulaic Latin learned in the notarial schools of central Italy, these protocols (together with the thousands of volumes compiled by his colleagues) constitute a fundamental source for the history of Florentine society in the Renaissance.

Notaries played an important role in the legalistic and litigious society of Florence. They were employed by people from every social stratum to draw up wills, property transactions, dowry contracts, and settlements of disputes. They also found employment in the civic bureaucracy, drafting legislation and keeping minutes of council meetings and court records. Though not as highly regarded professionally or as well trained as lawyers with doctoral degrees, they were men of learning who could read and write Latin and possessed some knowledge of the law. Together with lawyers, they belonged to one of the city's most prestigious guilds, the *arte dei giu-*

dici e notai. Like Ser Filippo, who was born in Castelfranco near Arezzo, many of these notaries were natives of rural districts adjacent to the city. They moved to Florence, seeking their fortunes in that metropolis of 50,000 inhabitants. While the majority achieved only modest success in their profession, some like Coluccio Salutati (d. 1406) gained wealth and renown as high civic officials and humanistic scholars.

In the mid-1440s Ser Filippo obtained an appointment as notary for the archiepiscopal curia. Thereafter, his clients included Archbishop Antoninus and his vicar general, the canons in the cathedral chapter, monastic foundations, and individual priests and monks. For these clerics and the religious communities to which they belonged, Ser Filippo drafted petitions for benefices, recorded the details of property transactions, and made transcriptions of the documents pertaining to judicial cases brought before the archiepiscopal court.

In his role as notary for the court, Ser Filippo compiled the dossier of an extraordinary case that was tried before Antoninus and his vicar general in the summer and autumn of 1455. The plaintiff was Lusanna, the daughter of an artisan named Maestro Benedetto di Girolamo, and the widow of a linen-cloth manufacturer, Andrea di Antonio Nucci. In his deposition to the court, Lusanna's procurator (her legal representative) asserted that after the death of her first husband, she had married Giovanni di Ser Lodovico della Casa, a wealthy merchant and scion of a prominent Florentine family. Though disputes over the legality of marriages were not uncommon in Italian church courts in the fifteenth century, this case was highly unusual. Comprising some three hundred pages, the dossier is the most detailed and comprehensive record of a Florentine judicial process, in either secular or ecclesiastical courts, that has survived from the fifteenth century. Included in the dossier is the testimony of twenty-nine witnesses from a wide variety of social and economic backgrounds: aristocrats, artisans and their wives, apprentices and servants, peasants from the countryside, a Franciscan friar.

The lengthy, richly textured case illuminates many features of Florentine social experience. The dispute focused primarily upon the question of marriage, specifically, whether Giovanni and Lusanna had been legally wed. But inevitably that issue was linked to the emotional bonds between the lovers, the sentiments that they felt and expressed, and the reaction of their kinfolk and neighbors. On such themes as love, marriage, and the moral conventions governing relations between the sexes, the testimony of the witnesses is very instructive. Many of their voices were rarely heard in this world dominated by rich and powerful men: six of the thirty-one who testified in the archiepiscopal court were women, and nineteen others were from the lower ranks of Florentine society. The disparity in social status between Giovanni and Lusanna was a critical issue in the dispute, evoking a variety of reactions from the witnesses. The case raises important questions about Florence's social hierarchy: its structure, its gradations, its rules. It also documents judicial procedure in an Italian ecclesiastical court, including a bitter fight over a jurisdictional issue between the archbishop and the *podestà*, the official responsible for criminal justice in the city. As often happened in this tightly knit community, a private quarrel escalated into a sensitive political issue, which may have created a rift in the Medicean party that governed Florence. The resonances of the dispute between two lovers extended far beyond their own lives and fortunes; its effects were felt throughout the social, political, and religious world of Renaissance Florence.

Born in 1420 (the precise date is unknown), Lusanna grew up in her father's house in the parish of San Marco, not far from the convent that later became renowned as the headquarters of the Dominican friar Girolamo Savonarola. Her father, Benedetto di Girolamo, was an immigrant from Dalmatia who earned his livelihood as a tailor. By his first wife, a native of the Casentino east of Florence, he had five children who were alive in 1433: Filippo, Antonio, Marco (who became a priest), Israello, and Lusanna. Benedetto's first wife died sometime after Lusanna's birth, and he then married a woman named Bartolomea (called Mea), the daughter of Domenico Fiocho, by whom he had three children: Girolamo, Caterina, and Domenico. Though not a native Florentine, Benedetto was quite successful in his business. He was described by artisans who knew him

4

as a worthy guildsman who practiced his trade honestly and competently. In 1433 he listed his property in his tax report (*catasto*): his residence on the Via del Cocomero (now the Via Ricasoli); two farms in the Mugello, a rural area north of Florence; and investments in the commune's funded debt, the *Monte*. For an artisan, this was a substantial bloc of property, considerably larger than the average patrimony of Florentine artisans and shopkeepers. When Benedetto arranged in November 1436 for the marriage of his daughter Lusanna to a linen-cloth maker, Andrea Nucci, he provided her with a sizeable dowry of 250 florins. This figure was considerably larger than the average marriage portion for daughters of artisan parents. Since Lusanna was the only girl among Benedetto's four children by his first wife, he could afford to give her a substantial dowry. Lusanna's husband, Andrea, was the son of a prosperous baker, Antonio Nucci, whose income came from his trade and from the rental of three bakeries in the San Lorenzo area.

Although Lusanna's father and her husband, Andrea, were more prosperous than most of their peers, their world was sharply defined by their artisanal, petit-bourgeois traditions and lifestyles. Florentine artisans were typically attached to a particular parish or neighborhood where they—and their parents and grandparents before them—had forged bonds of marriage, friendship, and clientage with their neighbors. Within those social enclaves they arranged marriages, selected godparents for their children, formed business partnerships, and established clienteles for their shops. Being a foreigner, Benedetto did not belong to an elaborate kinship structure that would have provided support for many of his fellow artisans. Still, he could expect to receive help and counsel from individuals linked to him by guild membership, marriage, godparentage, and friendship. Though no concrete evidence survives to support this conclusion, it is likely, too, that Benedetto found patrons and benefactors among the wealthy and socially prominent families in his neighborhood.

Concerning Lusanna's childhood and adolescence in her father's house, the documentary record is silent. We do not know when her mother died; we can only surmise that she was about seven when her father married Mea, who was eleven years older than her stepdaughter, and began to rear a second family. She was seventeen when Benedetto arranged for her marriage to Andrea Nucci, aged twenty-nine, in November 1436. The marriage contract and the dowry settlement were redacted by a notary, Ser Piero da Vulparia. Lusanna's husband lived in the Via San Gallo, adjacent to the Canto della Macina and not far from the church of San Lorenzo, which in those years was being rebuilt with Medici money under the supervision of the architect Filippo Brunelleschi. From her father's house to that of her husband was, for Lusanna, a move of a few hundred meters; after 1436 she was still living in very familiar surroundings. She would have attended religious services in San Lorenzo but also

6

A merchant in his shop

in the conventual church of San Marco, occupied since 1436 by the Dominican Observants and inhabited by Fra Antoninus from 1437 until his promotion to archbishop in 1444. Lusanna was also a frequent visitor to the Servite church of Santissima Annunziata, with its famed image of the Annunciation, a particular object of veneration of Florentine women hoping to become pregnant. While visiting one of these churches in the early 1440s, Lusanna was seen and admired by a young Florentine merchant, Giovanni della Casa, who lived in her parish of San Lorenzo and whose passion for the beautiful young woman is a central theme of this story.

Though born and reared in the parish of San Lorenzo, only a five-minute walk from Lusanna's residence, Giovanni della Casa inhabited a very different world. His family, the Della Casa, belonged to the upper echelons of Florentine society. His kinfolk associated with the Medici, the richest and most potent house in the city, and with other prominent families in the quarter of San Giovanni: Cerretani, Carnesecchi, Martelli, Ginori, Ciai. Giovanni was born in 1420; his father, Ser Lodovico della Casa, was a notary frequently employed by civic magistracies to record their formal acts. Ser Lodovico's tax declaration for 1430 listed his eight children: Francesco (a monk), Piera (a nun), Antonio, Ruggiero, Lotto, Alessandra, Jacopo, and Giovanni. He owned substantial real estate in the Mugello region north of Florence as well as a large bloc of shares in the commune's funded debt. Giovanni's older brothers were all engaged in international trade and banking. Antonio had been an employee of the Medici bank in Rome in the 1430s; in 1439 he established his own company there in partnership with Jacopo Donati. Another brother, Ruggiero, was the head of Medici business operations in Geneva from 1433 until 1447. Giovanni was a salaried employee in Antonio's Rome company in 1439; sometime after 1444 he returned to Florence permanently to work in his brother's firm. By 1451 he and his brother Jacopo were the major partners of that banking and mercantile enterprise. Giovanni was also active in the manufacture of silk cloth in Florence, an expanding and profitable industry in these years. His tax declaration of 1458, submitted jointly with Jacopo, reveals that with gross assets of 5,800 florins the two brothers ranked among the most affluent citizens of their quarter of San Giovanni, though their wealth was modest by comparison with the huge fortune, calculated at 123,000 florins, of their neighbor Cosimo de' Medici.

As a young bachelor in the 1440s, Giovanni lived in his parents' home in the parish of San Lorenzo, when he was not away—in Rome, Venice, Milan, Naples—on business trips. He would not have thought seriously about marriage until he was thirty and had established himself in the competitive world of international trade and banking. Young men of his wealth and social rank were in great demand as potential husbands for Florentine girls of aristocratic lineage, whose fathers were willing to give large dowries (1,000 to 2,000 florins and more) so that their daughters could marry honorably. No evidence has survived to identify Giovanni della Casa as a prospective husband for the hundreds of teenage girls who were in the marriage market in the 1440s and 1450s. Some of these maidens and their parents and relatives might have seen Giovanni at wedding celebrations and other *feste* where upper-class Florentines met, exchanged greetings, and dined together. But Giovanni's interest in marriage subsided when, in 1442 or 1443, he met Lusanna (then married for five years), with whom he fell passionately in love and who, for twelve years, was the focus of his emotional and erotic interest.

Archbishop Antoninus (Antonio di Ser Niccolò Pierozzi) was born and reared in the same neighborhood near San Marco as Lusanna and Giovanni. In 1427 his widowed mother lived on the Via del Cocomero, the street also inhabited by Lusanna's father, Benedetto. Antoninus's father, Ser Niccolò Pierozzi, was a notary of modest social status. Antoninus entered the Dominican order in 1404, living in Observant convents in Cortona, Foligno, Fiesole, and Naples. From 1430 to 1437 he worked in Rome as an official of the Roman curia under Pope Eugenius IV. In 1437 he returned to his native city as a member of the newly established Observant convent of San Marco. Perhaps recalling Antoninus's legal and administrative expertise as an auditor of the Roman Rota (the high court of the papal curia), Eugenius IV chose him to be archbishop of Florence in 1444. Antoninus was the most effective and influential head of the Tuscan archdiocese in the fifteenth century, indeed, one of the most illustrious prelates of his age. His years of service in the papal court had given him a perspective on the problems of ecclesiastical government that his conventual experience could not have provided. He was a reformer who worked hard to raise the moral and educational standards of his clergy and thus to improve the quality of spiritual guidance for the laity of his archdiocese. In his *Summa theologica*, which he wrote as a pastoral guide for his clergy, he revealed his sensible and pragmatic approach to the problems of living as a Christian in the secularized world of fifteenth-century Italy.

The Florentine bookseller and author Vespasiano da Bisticci had known Antoninus before and during his elevation to the archiepiscopal see. In his biographical sketch of the friar, he commented on his piety, for which he was well known, and on the austerity of his life in the archiepiscopal palace, so different from the opulence that characterized the life-style of most prelates in the Roman curia and the great Italian sees. So revered was the archbishop in Florence and throughout the peninsula that "when he passed along a road, everyone fell to his knees to honor him." According to Vespasiano, Antoninus was the most approachable of pastors; the doors of the palace were open to all who wished to consult him. Florentine merchants asked him for advice on the legality of business contracts and certain types of investments. Popes and prelates as well as lesser folk sought his counsel on points of canon law and problems of conscience. In cases that came before his tribunal, he was never influenced by the reputation or status of the parties. Vespasiano described how Cosimo de' Medici once asked the archbishop to rule in his favor on a case before his court. Antoninus told Florence's most powerful citizen that "it was not necessary [to petition him], for if he was in the right, justice would be rendered to him, as it would be to the lowliest man in Florence." As a judge, Antoninus was knowledgeable, fair, and incorruptible; Vespasiano added that he had chosen as his deputy and vicar general a man (Messer Raffaello de' Primadicis) as honest and virtuous as himself.

A testimonial to Antoninus's reputation in Florence was his election on 19 April 1455 by the Florentine government to head the republic's delegation to Pope Calixtus III to congratulate him on his recent election to the Holy See. The archbishop returned from this diplomatic assignment on 21 June. On 27 June, when he was in his palace adjacent to the cathedral, he was given a letter (*breve*) from the pope. The letter had been brought to the palace by Antonio di Benedetto, Lusanna's brother who was serving as her procurator. Dated 4 June from Rome, the letter read: "Our beloved daughter in Christ, Lusanna di Benedetto, a Florentine woman, has informed us that, despite a marriage legally contracted between herself and a certain Giovanni di Lodovico della Casa, he has married another Florentine woman in a public ceremony with an exchange of vows and rings and with other customary solemnities." Calixtus's letter instructed Antoninus to investigate the case and, if Lusanna's allegations were found to be true, to dissolve the second marriage, compel Giovanni to accept Lusanna as his legal spouse, and impose certain penalties upon him for contracting a bigamous marriage.

Antoninus had actually learned about Lusanna's complaint more than a month before he received the papal *breve*. An entry in Ser Filippo Mazzei's protocol dated 15 May 1455 describes the interrogation by the archbishop and his vicar general of Fra Felice Asini, a Franciscan friar in the convent of Santa Croce. The subject of this inquest was the alleged marriage between Lusanna, widow of Andrea Nucci, and Giovanni della Casa. Fra Felice testified under oath that he had officiated at this ceremony. The case was thus known to the archbishop when he traveled to Rome as a member of the Florentine embassy to congratulate Calixtus III on his elevation. Antoninus may indeed have discussed Lusanna's complaint with officials in Rome, some of whom he would have known from his years of service in the curia. It is possible that one of the Florentine ambassadors or a member of the entourage had acted as Lusanna's agent in Rome to obtain the papal letter instructing Antoninus to investigate the case. The archbishop's personal interest in Lusanna's process is well documented in Ser Filippo's protocol. He presided over several court sessions; he personally interrogated witnesses; he was almost certainly involved in formulating the final decision of his court.

THE
HISTORY OF
A RELATIONSHIP

LUSANNA'S STORY

On 14 July 1455 Lusanna's procurator, Messer Stefano di Francesco of Prato, submitted to the archiepiscopal court a document comprising fifteen chapters (*capitoli*) describing his client's relationship with Giovanni della Casa. He later called thirteen witnesses to testify in the court concerning the specific points in his brief. Of this number, three were Lusanna's close kin: her brother Antonio, her sister-in-law Cosa, her stepmother, Mea. Antonio's seventeen-year-old servant, Ammannato Ammannati, who had lived with his master since 1450, was also called to testify, as was the Franciscan friar Fra Felice Asini, who officiated at the wedding ceremony. Finally, seven peasants who lived near Antonio's farm outside Florence were brought into the city to make their depositions in the case.

Lusanna, so witnesses testified, was a strikingly beautiful woman (*valde formosa et pulcra*) who had attracted the attention of Giovanni della Casa while her husband Andrea was still alive.

Antonio recalled that Giovanni would follow his sister in the streets and would approach her in markets and churches "as lovers are wont to do," even though the chaste Lusanna gave him no encouragement. After Andrea's death in January 1453, Giovanni's amorous signals became more pronounced, as he walked back and forth in front of Antonio's house, where the widowed Lusanna was then living. Concerned about the reputation of his sister and his nubile daughters, Antonio sent a mutual friend, Giuliana, the wife of Niccolò Magaldi, to appeal to Giovanni to cease his perambulations. Giovanni then came to see Antonio and told him of his love for Lusanna. Antonio, however, would not consider the possibility of an illicit relationship, and he insisted that Giovanni "give her a ring," that is, that he marry Lusanna. When Giovanni finally consented to a wedding ceremony, Antonio argued for the presence of a notary, who customarily officiated at Florentine weddings and redacted the nuptial contract. On this point, however, Giovanni della Casa demurred. His father, Ser Lodovico, would disinherit him if he learned about his son's matrimony, which must therefore be kept secret. "What, then, are we to do?" asked Antonio. Giovanni suggested that he ask his friend Fra Felice Asini to officiate at the wedding, and that proposal was accepted by Antonio and Lusanna.

Certain features of this ceremony were unusual if not unique: it was celebrated only four months after the bride was widowed; it was clandestine; it did not involve the payment of a

Visit of a suitor

dowry. Given its peculiar character and the fact that its occurrence was later denied by Giovanni, it is necessary to describe the event in detail from the recollections of the main witnesses: Antonio, Mea, Cosa, and Fra Felice Asini. Giovanni had first sent the son of Niccolò Magaldi to Santa Croce to ask Fra Felice to come to Antonio's house. When the friar ignored the request, Niccolò himself went to the cloister to escort him and a young novice (*fraticino*) to the wedding. They arrived at Antonio's house after sunset, and the members of the wedding party were already at dinner. Present for the nuptials were the principals, Giovanni and Lusanna; Antonio and his wife, Cosa; his stepmother, Mea; Giuliana and Niccolò Magaldi; Antonio's three daughters; and five Magaldi children. The young people were barred from direct participation in the wedding ceremony "for honesty's sake," but they were allowed to watch from the stairs leading to the upper floor.

Fra Felice testified that he was invited to eat, and when the meal was finished, Giovanni said to him, "We have sent for you because I wish to take Lusanna for my wife. We request your presence, and we would like you to say a few words appropriate to the occasion." The members of the wedding party then formed a circle around the friar and the couple. Fra Felice formally asked Giovanni whether he wished to take Lusanna as his wife, and he replied, "Yes." The friar repeated the question to Lusanna, who also responded affirmatively. Giovanni took a ring from his left hand and placed it on Lusanna's finger, while her brother held her hand. The bridegroom exchanged kisses with Mea, with Cosa, and finally with Antonio. After Giovanni presented gifts to Lusanna's relatives, he shared a flask of wine with the members of the wedding party. Giovanni and Lusanna then went into a bedroom on the upper floor to consummate their marriage. Since the night curfew was in force, Fra Felice and his *fraticino* spent the night in Antonio's bed while the host and his wife slept in another room.

Did this wedding ceremony actually occur, or was it, as Giovanni della Casa's procurator alleged, a fabrication constructed by Lusanna and her kin to trap his client and to subvert justice? Aware of the crucial importance of the ceremony to the case, the archbishop and his vicar general pressed the witnesses to search their memories for concrete details. On what day, at what time, did the wedding take place? What was eaten at the dinner prior to the ceremony? What did the bride and groom wear? What kind of ring did Giovanni give to Lusanna? The witnesses were in general agreement about the progression of events from the moment that Fra Felice arrived until the hosts and guests went to bed. But they did not remember every detail. Cosa could not recall the particular day in May when the wedding occurred two years before, though she remembered that it was not a feast day. The women described Lusanna's green gown in lavish detail, though they were vague about Giovanni's costume. Cosa testified that Giovanni's ring was gold with an inlaid stone, but she could not identify the jewel. The fuzziness of memory about details lends credence to this account by the five witnesses as does, too, the improvisational, ad hoc character of the wedding. Had the story been fabricated, it would have been a tidier account.

Except for Fra Felice, the only independent witnesses (neither relatives nor dependents) at the wedding were Niccolò and Giuliana Magaldi, and they were called by Giovanni della Casa to support his argument. Since at Giovanni's behest the marriage was not publicized in the neighborhood, no witnesses outside the family could testify about the relationship between Giovanni and Lusanna. When she appeared in public Lusanna continued to wear widow's garb, though in the privacy of Antonio's house she dressed as a married woman. Giovanni did not live continuously with Lusanna after their wedding, though he did spend occasional nights with her. Antonio's wife, Cosa, testified that he would call out whenever he entered the house, "Where is my wife (*Ove è moglia mia*)?" and that he brought grain, wine, and oil to the house. He also arranged to buy a slave girl named Caterina to serve Lusanna, though the contract of sale was made in her name.

In Florence Giovanni and Lusanna kept their marriage secret, but, for a brief moment in the countryside outside the city walls, they felt liberated from the constraints of their clandestine relationship. The site was Antonio's farm, located in the *pieve* of San Piero a Pitiana, some fifteen miles east of Florence, near Rignano sull'Arno. In August 1454 Antonio and his house-hold, including Lusanna, went to their country house to escape the city heat and enjoy the rustic life in this bucolic setting. Five local peasants tes-tified that they saw Giovanni and Lusanna to-gether at Antonio's villa, which was called Ca-pello, and that the couple was accepted by the residents of the district as man and wife. They were seen walking together in the fields, collect-ing salad greens for a meal; one witness reported that they sat together at dinner in Antonio's villa "as if they were husband and wife." Another wit-ness stated that Lusanna did not wear a widow's veil but a brown tunic appropriate for a married woman. Giovanni and Lusanna went together to a feast in the house of a neighbor to celebrate the birth of a male child. With Antonio and Cosa they made a pilgrimage to the nearby monastery of Vallombrosa, the men on horseback, the women on foot. In this summer *villeggiatura* Lu-sanna was able to enjoy, for the first time since her first husband had died, the satisfaction of being a married woman and being recognized as such by the members of the rural community. One wit-ness, Antonio Tronchi, described a scene that cap-tured her mood: "He saw Lusanna go to meet Giovanni and take his hand and greet him joy-fully, and Giovanni responded in like manner to her." When Lusanna could not remove from her finger a ring that Giovanni had given her, he told her to wear it. When she reminded him that he did not wish her to appear in public as a married

Love in the country

woman, he replied, "It is well that it [our marriage] be known."

Eight months later, Lusanna was shocked to learn that Giovanni had contracted a marriage with Marietta, the fifteen-year-old daughter of Piero di Cardinale Rucellai, whose family was among the most distinguished in the city. The marriage had been arranged sometime after Giovanni's father had died in February 1455. The death of Ser Lodovico should have been the occasion for Giovanni's public acknowledgment of his marriage to Lusanna; it was instead the prelude to his renunciation of that marital bond. In his affidavit to the archiepiscopal court, Lusanna's procurator asserted that on several occasions she had appealed to Giovanni to abandon his bigamous relationship and recognize her as his legitimate spouse. He had refused her requests, thus violating the sacred canons and the sacrament of matrimony, gravely harming Lusanna, and endangering his own soul. In view of his obduracy Lusanna was forced to appeal to the ecclesiastical authorities for the reaffirmation of her marital status and the vindication of her rights.

GIOVANNI'S STORY

The image of Lusanna as an honest and virtuous woman was sharply challenged by Giovanni's legal representatives in the court and by the witnesses called to support his cause. According to their allegations, Lusanna had had sexual rela-

25

tions with several men in her neighborhood, even while her husband Andrea was alive. One of her lovers was Giovanni della Casa. His procurators admitted that Giovanni and Lusanna had had a sexual relationship since 1443, but they denied that the two had ever been married. Their argument was stated most bluntly in their response to the ninth *capitolo* of Lusanna's affidavit: "Motivated by lust, Lusanna desired to have carnal relations with him [Giovanni], for he was young and well endowed . . . and Lusanna was infatuated with him while her husband Andrea was alive and after his death." Giovanni's procurators were thus prepared to admit their client was a voluptuary and, indeed, was guilty of adultery. By so doing, they sought to blacken Lusanna's reputation, depicting her as no better than a prostitute, as someone whose social condition and morals would disqualify her from marriage with a Della Casa.

Giovanni's procurators summoned three witnesses from notable families—Giovanni Panciatichi, Giuliano Gondi, and Carlo Guasconi—to testify concerning the exalted social rank of the Della Casa and Giovanni's reputation as a prosperous and successful merchant. But most of those called to testify for his side were Lusanna's neighbors and erstwhile friends from the same artisan community to which her father and her first husband had belonged. These included Niccolò and Giuliana Magaldi and their two sons, all of whom had allegedly been present at the wedding ceremony of Giovanni and Lusanna in May 1453.

In addition to Giuliana, three other women from the neighborhood—Fiora, the wife of Angelo dell'Opere; Tita, the wife of Piero Cavicciuli (a messenger in the Merchants' Court); and Guglielma, the widow of Nanni di Piero—were important sources of information about Lusanna and her domestic life. Their evidence is particularly informative concerning Lusanna's character and her motives, though the reliability of their testimony cannot be taken for granted. These women collected and reported neighborhood gossip about Lusanna, and in varying degrees their testimony revealed their personal bias against her.

Nearly all the eighteen witnesses called by Giovanni's procurators reported, either as a personal judgment or as public rumor (*publica vox et fama*), that Lusanna was a woman of low moral character. Thus, Giovanni Panciatichi: "She had a bad reputation on account of her love affairs and her vanities." Very conscious of her beauty (*vana et vaga*), she stared openly at men whom she encountered in the street, a violation of the social convention which decreed that respectable women should lower their gaze in public. According to these witnesses, her affair with Giovanni della Casa had begun as early as 1447 or 1448, some five years before her first husband's death. The lovers were seen together in public places and in private dwellings, and to certain of their acquaintances they confessed their love for each other. But rumors also circulated in the San Lorenzo neighborhood that Lusanna had lovers besides Giovanni. These were identified as Gio-

vanni Berardi, Giorgio Aldobrandini, and an un-
named youth who (so it was alleged) wounded
Giovanni in a quarrel over Lusanna. Niccolò
Magaldi asserted that he had heard a rumor that
horns (*cornia bestiarum*) had been nailed over the
door of the house inhabited by Andrea and Lusanna and that the husband had been publicly
called a cuckold (*becco*) by a neighbor. Andrea's
passivity in these circumstances is puzzling; he
was described by acquaintances as a competent
artisan who was remiss (*remissus*) in disciplining
his wife.

So much of the opinion concerning Lusanna's
character and reputation was based on hearsay
that one must exercise great caution in evaluating
it. But in the mass of testimony by neighbors
and acquaintances are accounts of two episodes
which are reported in such elaborate detail (and
corroborated by several witnesses) that the possibility of their fabrication seems remote. Piero
Cavicciuli, his wife, Tita, and their four children
lived in a house adjacent to that of Lusanna and
her first husband, Andrea, on the Via San Gallo.
Piero also had close ties with Giovanni della Casa,
who was the godfather of his children and had
occasionally hired him to weave silk cloth. At
some unspecified date (but possibly in 1443 or
1444), Lusanna had seen Giovanni and Piero together in the street. She later asked Piero to invite Giovanni to the Cavicciuli house, since she
wished to speak with him. The two met at a gate
that separated Lusanna's house from Piero's; they
conversed for nearly two hours. The next morn-

ing (so Tita testified), Giovanni returned to the Cavicciuli house before dawn. When the members of Lusanna's household had left for work, she passed through the gate into Piero's dwelling to meet Giovanni. They called Tita, who was weaving silk in a room on the floor below, and, in her presence and that of Tita's mother-in-law, Guglielma, Lusanna said to Giovanni while they held hands, "I want you to promise me that, if my [husband] Andrea dies, you will take me for your wife (*per moglie*) and I will be your spouse (*tua donna*)." Giovanni replied, "I will do it willingly (*di buona voglia*)." Tita then went back to her loom. When she returned upstairs, she found the two lovers lying on her bed, and she surmised that they had had carnal relations. According to her testimony, this was the first of several occasions when Giovanni and Lusanna used the Cavicciuli house for their assignations. On one occasion (her husband Piero testified), the family returned from a dinner with friends to find the two lovers in his and Tita's bed. "What the devil are you doing?" an irate Piero demanded. Lusanna replied, "Be patient; this is the situation"; she then asked Giovanni in Piero's presence to repeat his promise of matrimony.

A similar scene, described by Niccolò and Giuliana Magaldi and their sons Andrea and Antonio, took place in their house on the Via de' Pilastri in the parish of San Ambrogio. The Magaldi family had known Lusanna, her father, and her brother for nearly thirty years (Niccolò's sister had lived adjacent to their home on the Via del

Cocomero); their son Andrea had been employed in the workshop of Lusanna's first husband for eight years. In January of 1447 or 1448, Giuliana testified, Lusanna came to her house and said that she "wished to say four words to Giovanni della Casa" because she knew that Giuliana's husband wove silk cloth for Giovanni. Giuliana's initial response was negative, but when Lusanna persisted, she agreed to consult with her husband. Amenable to Lusanna's request, Niccolò brought Giovanni home the next evening and told him of Lusanna's desire. The next morning Giovanni came to the Magaldi house, as did Lusanna, who was accompanied by a four-year-old girl named Lavaggia. Then, Giuliana reported, "both went into the bedroom of Niccolò and Giuliana on the ground floor, and there they remained alone at their pleasure, and she [Giuliana] believed that they had sexual relations." Later the couple ascended to the living room on the second floor, and Giovanni sent Niccolò's son to buy some eggs, bread, and wine. While standing by the fire and holding hands, Lusanna said to Giovanni, "I will be your wife and you will be my husband; have you not so promised me?" When Giovanni agreed that he had made that commitment, an incredulous Giuliana asked Lusanna, "How can he be your husband? You would be risking [death by] fire to have two husbands." Lusanna replied, "It has been four years since he promised himself to me, and I to him." They then ate, went back to the bedroom, and remained there until dusk. This was one of several meetings between the lovers

An unexpected visit

in the Magaldi house where they retired to the bedroom and where, on one occasion, they were seen lying together on the bed by Andrea Magaldi, who had gone into the courtyard for water.

By persuading Giovanni to repeat his promise before two groups of witnesses, Lusanna may have believed that she was securing her future, but she also, inevitably, raised suspicions about her motives and actions when Andrea succumbed to an illness diagnosed as *la scesa* in January 1453. Andrea Magaldi, who had been employed in Andrea Nucci's shop, went to the funeral. There he heard the lament of a woman named Masa, a friend of the deceased. "*Oime*, my son, your heart must have been poisoned!" Andrea reported, too, that he had heard rumors in the neighborhood that his employer had died of poison. Giuliana Magaldi testified that she had met Lusanna a month after Andrea's death. Lusanna asked her when she had last seen Giovanni della Casa. "You know," she added, "that he promised to marry me if Andrea were to die." Giuliana then asked, "What have you done?" Lusanna told her that she had commissioned a girl to buy some silver (*ariento sodo*), which she ground up in a bowl and mixed with her husband's medicine. "So tell *that* to Giovanni," Lusanna allegedly told her friend.

This evidence by hostile witnesses was designed to depict Lusanna as a woman enslaved by her passions, whose carnal desires had impelled her to commit adultery and possibly even murder. None of the witnesses acknowledged that they had been present at, or had heard about, the

33

wedding that had allegedly taken place in Antonio di Benedetto's house in the spring of 1453. Three Magaldi witnesses who (according to Antonio, Mea, Cosa, and Fra Felice Asini) had been at the ceremony specifically denied that assertion. Andrea's death had not changed the nature of their relationship, which was, in the view of these witnesses, a sexual liaison and not a marital bond. Giovanni's servant Antonio of Borgo San Lorenzo testified that his master frequently visited Lusanna at night in her brother's house and slept with her there. He also reported that Lusanna, concerned for her reputation, instructed Giovanni to come only at night to her house.

The evidence of Giovanni's intentions concerning Lusanna is confused and ambiguous and perhaps reflects his own doubts. Whatever his earlier thoughts about the relationship, he had apparently decided by the winter of 1454–55 to disengage himself from Lusanna so that he would be free to marry another woman and raise a family. Giovanni's servant Antonio is the main source of information about his efforts to obtain a papal dispensation dissolving his marital bond to Lusanna. He testified that in December 1454 his master had brought back from Rome a papal bull releasing Giovanni from his commitment to Lusanna and authorizing him to contract another marriage. He had heard Giovanni describe the contents of the document to his brother Jacopo and his wife, and he had also seen the parchment in Giovanni's room. When, however, he was asked to bring the bull to the court, he exhibited a *breve* of Calixtus III concerning not Giovanni and Lusanna but "a process against a certain Fra Felice."

During these months Lusanna became increasingly aware of her precarious situation; her erratic behavior reflected her anxiety. She hoped that Giovanni would recognize her openly as his wife, and, to placate him, she continued to welcome him to her home and her bed. But this strategy was not successful, and she felt increasingly vulnerable, isolated, and uncertain about her future. To Monna Tita she appealed for help to persuade Giovanni to honor his obligation to her. Another witness, Monna Fiora, reported a conversation overheard between Lusanna and her brother Antonio in December 1454. "You have humiliated us," Antonio cried, "and have placed a mark of shame on me and on your sister." A remorseful Lusanna replied, "You are right; kill me!" to which Antonio responded brutally, "Kill yourself!" When Antonio had left the house after that acrimonious exchange, Fiora asked Lusanna to explain the cause of the scandal. Giovanni had returned from Rome and had told her that he could not marry her. Fiora asked her if she had ever received a ring from him. When Lusanna replied in the negative, Fiora suggested a solution to the problem: Giovanni should promise not to contract a marriage for two years, during which time Lusanna and her sister would be wed, "and so your honor, and that of your sister, will be salvaged."

Soon after her husband Andrea died, prospective suitors for Lusanna's hand began to inquire about her availability, undoubtedly attracted by the knowledge that she had a dowry of 250 florins. Since Lusanna considered herself bound by her vows to Giovanni, she rebuffed these overtures. After the news of Giovanni's marriage to the Rucellai girl circulated through the San Marco neighborhood, brokers intensified their efforts to find a suitable partner for Lusanna. Bartolomeo Boni described his attempts to arrange a marriage between her and Giovanni di Ser Simone Strada, which broke down because Lusanna did not wish to live with a mother-in-law. The used-clothes dealer Mazza di Jacopo del Mazza was particularly assiduous in pressing the claims of his clients, though he noted that Lusanna was unwilling to commit herself to any agreement. Tita heard rumors that she was considering marriage offers from a notary, Ser Soletto, and a cloth weaver named Pierone. Other suitors were identified by Andrea Magaldi as Piero di Romolo Cecchi and "a young man from the Serragli family." Monna Fiora reported that she had been commissioned by Lusanna to ask friends of a certain Baldinaccio, reputed to be in love with her, whether he would be willing to contract a marriage. She discovered, however, that Baldinaccio's relatives were prepared to put him in jail to prevent it.

According to Giovanni's witnesses, the news of his marriage to Marietta Rucellai in April 1455 did not signal an immediate and total breach between him and Lusanna and her family. Giovanni encouraged her to find a spouse; the marriage broker Mazza reported that Giovanni was present, though in an adjacent room, when he first discussed prospective marriage partners with Lusanna and Antonio. Giovanni's servant Antonio testified that on 30 April, the feast day of Santa Croce, Giovanni came to Lusanna's house and dined with her. Arriving home later, her brother Antonio greeted Giovanni warmly and announced that Lusanna's marriage was being arranged by the broker Mazza. Giovanni and Lusanna then retired to her bedroom. The next morning Lusanna dismissed Giovanni's servant with the prophetic words, "I do not know if he will ever come back." That may have been their last meeting.

THE QUEST
FOR JUSTICE

The papal *breve* of 4 June 1455, received and recorded in Antoninus's court on 27 June, set in mo-
tion a lengthy and complex judicial process that
preoccupied the archbishop, his vicar general,
and the notary Ser Filippo throughout the summer and autumn of that year. As "judge and
apostolic commissioner" in the case, Antoninus
bore the primary responsibility for resolving the
dispute. But "knowing himself to be involved in
numerous and varied affairs of his archdiocese,"
he delegated authority to hear the case to Messer
Raffaello, a doctor of canon law. The vicar general and the curial notary, Ser Filippo Mazzei,
were continuously involved in the process, except for a brief interlude when Messer Raffaello
was away in Bologna. Antoninus took over the
process during his absence (4–18 July), and he
also joined Messer Raffaello and Ser Filippo in the
interrogation of witnesses. The main hall of the
archbishop's palace was the site of the formal
hearings in the case, with either Antoninus or
Messer Raffaello presiding "on the bench of justice." The witnesses were questioned in private,

either in the studies of the two clerics or in the nearby church of San Salvatore.

Antoninus was both knowledgeable and experienced in the canon law, as his *Summa theologica* amply demonstrates. As a judge in the Roman Rota, he had decided hundreds of cases, including, certainly, disputes over marriage contracts. The elaborate procedure followed by Antoninus and his vicar general was designed to serve justice and safeguard the rights of the litigants. Lusanna's procurator was a cleric, a chaplain in the cathedral, Messer Stefano of Prato. Giovanni della Casa was represented by Ser Piero Migliorelli and Ser Domenico da Figline, both of whom had lengthy experience as curial notaries. Their activities in this process, well documented in Ser Filippo's protocols, show clearly that they had mastered the intricacies of canon-law procedure and were adept at manipulating the rules for their clients' advantage.

The slow and laborious grinding of these particular wheels of justice is recorded in painstaking detail by Ser Filippo Mazzei. He made copies of each legal move by the contending parties, identified the presiding officer of the court, and noted the date and hour of each action taken by the procurators and the judges. While the protocol record traces carefully the steps of court procedure—the filing of affidavits, the challenges to these documents, the judges' decisions—it provides few clues to the legal theory that underlay the process and, specifically, the decisions of Antoninus and his vicar general.

Arguing a case

Immediately upon the receipt of the papal *breve* instructing Antoninus to investigate Lusanna's complaint, Giovanni della Casa was notified by curial messenger and ordered to appear in court to respond to the charge. On 30 June Giovanni's procurator Ser Domenico da Figline presented the first of several challenges (*exceptiones*) to the process. Lusanna's complaint should be dismissed, he argued, because she had not authorized it. Motivated solely by greed, her brother Antonio was the instigator of the cause. To find out the truth of the matter, Ser Domenico requested that the vicar general personally interrogate Lusanna, but for reasons not specified in the record Messer Raffaello rejected the proposal. When on the next day, 1 July, Messer Stefano of Prato asked for a copy of Ser Domenico's affidavit, the latter argued that his mandate to serve as Lusanna's procurator was not valid. On this legal point the vicar general supported Ser Domenico and ordered Messer Stefano to return on the following day with a proper mandate. He was also given two days to prepare a response to Ser Domenico's rebuttal.

On 2 July Messer Stefano submitted to the court an affidavit responding to the arguments made by Giovanni's procurator to quash the case against his client. Those arguments were, according to Messer Stefano, "empty, vague, varied, frivolous, uncertain and indeterminate, inane, defective, obscure, general and unspecific," and therefore unworthy of consideration. Considering each point made in the *exceptiones* submitted

43

by Ser Piero Migliorelli, Messer Stefano asserted
that the pope's charge to Antoninus to investigate Lusanna's complaint was legitimate, that her
brother Antonio was fully qualified to present it
to the court, and that the claims made by him on
Lusanna's behalf would be proven by witnesses.
Five days later, on 7 July, Ser Piero submitted yet
another cluster of legal objections. He repeated
his earlier argument that Lusanna's *libellus* was defective, being too vague, unspecific, and poorly
formulated. Moreover, he insisted, Messer Stefano was not qualified to be Lusanna's procurator,
since he was not, as he claimed, a doctor of law
nor had he ever served as a procurator in cases
brought before the episcopal courts of Florence
and Fiesole. Finally, Ser Piero asked Antoninus,
then presiding over the court, to require Lusanna,
"who possesses no property," to provide a guar-
antee that she or someone on her behalf could pay
the legal expenses incurred by his client and by
the court in the event that she lost her case. Antoninus did not rule immediately on these objections but agreed to consider them and to accept
those that were "valid in law, otherwise not." He
further stipulated that the procurators for both
sides should be prepared to continue their arguments in the case within eight days.

A week after Lusanna's brother had presented
the papal *breve* to the archbishop, Antoninus was
involved in a bitter imbroglio with Florence's *podestà*, Messer Giovanni della Porta of Novara, a
knight and a doctor of civil law. Messer Giovanni
was both police official and judicial magistrate,
presiding over the city's most important secular

44

court. In response to a private denunciation, his court had launched an investigation of the alleged poisoning of Lusanna's first husband, Andrea Nucci. The charge had been made either by Giovanni or by an accomplice to intimidate Lusanna and perhaps force her to withdraw her case in the archbishop's court. Giuliana Magaldi later testified that Giovanni had visited her in the church of Santa Maria del Campo prior to her appearance and had counseled her to be truthful in her testimony.

On 4 July Antoninus sent a letter to the *podestà* requesting him to cease his investigation of the alleged poisoning of Andrea. Perhaps the "generous knight and learned doctor" was not aware that Lusanna had earlier brought a case against Giovanni in his court. Were the *podestà* to continue his criminal investigation, it would inevitably be prejudicial to Lusanna's rights. The tone of the first letter and a second, sent a day later, was polite; that of a third (dispatched on 15 July) was stern. We have been informed, Antoninus wrote, that you have ignored our request, and, instead of abandoning the investigation against Lusanna, you have proceeded to interrogate witnesses in the case. You are hereby warned that unless you desist immediately, you will incur the penalty of excommunication. Once the marriage case is decided in the archiepiscopal court, Antoninus concluded, the *podestà* would be free to continue his investigation of the alleged poisoning. In these letters Antoninus did not state explicitly the premise underlying his position: that ecclesiastical justice had priority over its secular coun-

45

terpart and that in any jurisdictional dispute the lay judge must defer to the clerical.

Antoninus and the knight from Novara were soon embroiled in a rancorous quarrel that threatened to disturb the always tenuous balance of church and state in Florence. The escalation of the conflict was signaled by the curial messenger Francesco di Biagio, who reported to the archbishop on his attempts to deliver the second letter to the *podestà*:

This evening about the 14th hour . . . he [the messenger] took the letter to the lord *podestà*, then at table surrounded by his judges and officials. When the messenger told the *podestà* that he was bringing letters from the archbishop, . . . he did not wish to receive them. He [the *podestà*] said, "Go to the *podestà* who is in the [adjacent] room." The messenger replied, "You are the *podestà*; I know you, and I have always given you the other letters." And while he was standing there, a young man appeared dressed in curial robes and bearing a sword, pretending to be the *podestà*. This page accepted the letters from the messenger, . . . who said, "Take this letter and the other that the lord archbishop sent." Then he who pretended to be the *podestà* took the letter, opened it, and speaking to himself pretended to read it. And when the messenger was preparing to leave the hall, those standing about talking and laughing called him back and returned the letter to him. And the one dressed in the *podestà*'s garb said, "Go and return these letters, and tell the lord archbishop that he may do whatever pleases him."

The day after the archbishop's courier was treated with such contempt, on 16 July, Antoninus sent another letter to the *podestà*. He accused the magistrate of insulting him personally by the charade staged by his entourage; he condemned his persistent refusal to cease the criminal investigation of Andrea Nucci's death. For these offenses, which Antoninus interpreted as violations of his judicial authority, the archbishop formally summoned the *podestà* to appear at his court before sunset to be present at the reading of the sentence of excommunication. After this letter was drafted by Ser Filippo, it was sealed with the imprint of the archbishop's ring and given to the courier for delivery to the *podestà*. The messenger had no more success in fulfilling his mission than on the previous day. In the *podestà*'s palace a page informed him that Messer Giovanni was at dinner and could not be disturbed. Scanning the letter, he returned it to the courier and said to him, "Take these letters back and do not come here again; if you do, you will suffer." Undeterred by the rebuff, Antoninus sent the letter back in the custody of a cathedral canon, Messer Niccolò Corbizzi, accompanied by two priests and a servant. They were also frustrated in their mission since, they were told, the *podestà* had retired for the night. Antoninus then made his final move. He dispatched a priest named Marco, accompanied by a servant, with instructions either to deliver all the letters to the *podestà* or to nail them to the door of his palace. They were duly affixed to the gate, and after dusk Antoninus formally pronounced the sentence of excommunication against Messer Giovanni della Porta of Novara.

The *podestà* was not so insensitive as to be

wholly oblivious to this threat from the formidable archbishop. His legal staff formulated a written response to the arguments contained in Antoninus's letters; it was delivered to the archiepiscopal palace by the *podestà*'s procurator Ser Battista of Novara. The document asserted categorically that the accusations made by the archbishop against the *podestà* were wholly without merit. Messer Giovanni was legally entitled, indeed required by communal statutes, to investigate the alleged poisoning of Andrea Nucci. If he did not proceed in the case, he would be guilty of malfeasance. Ignoring the receptions that he and his staff had given to Antoninus's letters and couriers, the *podestà* insisted that he had never acted "in derogation of your dignity." He described himself as a faithful and obedient member of the church. In conclusion he requested the archbishop to cancel the sentence of excommunication, which was both illegal and unmerited. Antoninus instructed Ser Filippo Mazzei to make a copy of the *podestà*'s letter in his protocol, but he refused to accept the document in his court.

The excommunication of the *podestà*, the city's chief secular magistrate, was an embarrassment to the government since it raised doubts about the legality of his judicial acts. But how to resolve this dispute between two proud and stubborn men, each determined to defend his prerogatives? The impasse continued for more than six weeks before a compromise was achieved. In a meeting with its two collegiate bodies on 4 September, the Signoria, the commune's chief executive body, instructed the *podestà* to cease his investigation of Lusanna's alleged complicity in her husband's death. "They . . . have decided that the evidence in this inquisition should not be recognized, and therefore they have instructed the lord *podestà* to proceed no further . . . in this case, the record of which should be expunged from the protocols." Such intervention by the Signoria in cases before the *podestà*'s court was not uncommon in Florence; the magistrate could obey the order without feeling that his honor or his authority had been compromised. The archbishop was then able to lift the sentence of excommunication against Messer Giovanni, since his preeminent authority in this case had been implicitly recognized.

On 18 July, before the final resolution of the jurisdictional dispute, Antoninus again delegated authority over Lusanna's case to his vicar general, who had just returned from Bologna. On that day Giovanni's procurator Ser Domenico da Figline submitted a lengthy and detailed rebuttal to Lusanna's contention that she and Giovanni had been legally married. That Giovanni had been acquainted with Lusanna Ser Domenico did not deny. He admitted that since 1443 Lusanna had been Giovanni's concubine. But in that time, he insisted, no marriage ceremony had ever been celebrated, although he did concede that on two occasions (in November 1443 and January 1448) Giovani had promised before witnesses to marry his mistress if her husband were to die. These were the facts of the relationship that Ser Dome-

49

nico intended to prove by the testimony of witnesses. But in defending his client he also used the argument of probability. Giovanni was young, handsome, virile, and rich; Lusanna was old (at least forty, he claimed), she was sterile, and her social condition was vastly inferior to that of her lover. A marriage between two individuals of such unequal backgrounds was improbable, indeed, unthinkable. "He [Giovanni] is more noble, his family more distinguished, he is wealthier and much younger. Though for a long time he did have carnal relations with her to the point of satiation, it is not credible that he would ever have accepted her as his wife, for he would have married a prostitute to the grave dishonor of himself and his family." Ser Domenico again appealed to Messer Raffaello to interrogate Lusanna under oath, "as the best informed [witness]" concerning the case.

On 29 July Lusanna's procurator, Messer Stefano, presented his response to these arguments, which he described as false in fact and defective in law. In addition to this general characterization of Ser Domenico's affidavit, Messer Stefano also responded point by point to the objections raised by his opponent. While conceding that Lusanna's social condition was inferior to Giovanni's, he maintained that such disparity in marriage partners was not uncommon in Florence. Beautiful Florentine women of lowly origins often married men who were their social superiors and who did not insist on a dowry from their brides. For a marriage to be legal, it was not necessary that the

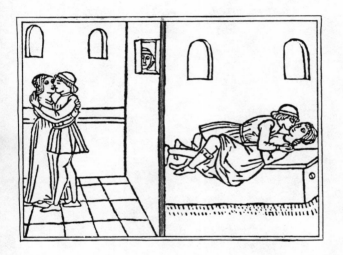

Intimate scenes

parties be equal with respect to "age, beauty, power, social rank, wealth, and family" or that the woman be fecund. It was sufficient that the two parties agreed freely to the marriage bond in the presence of witnesses. Finally, in response to the charge that Lusanna was a promiscuous woman, Messer Stefano stated categorically that, during her marriage to Andrea and later as his widow, she was "a chaste and honest woman, and as such was so regarded." She would never have permitted Giovanni or any other man except her husband to fondle her or know her carnally, "for in truth she was always guarded and protected by her husband Andrea."

Upon receipt of the affidavit, the vicar general instructed the procurators for both parties to return in ten days with their rebuttals to the arguments of their opponent. The next day, 30 July, Messer Stefano petitioned Messer Raffaello for a delay since his client Lusanna had left Florence "on account of the violence against her by the *podestà*." She was somewhere between Città di Castello and Borgo San Sepolcro, about fifty miles from the city, and he had to consult with her personally before he could present his next argument. Giovanni's procurator Ser Domenico objected to this petition as "frivolous, fraudulent, and false"; he urged the judge to proceed rapidly with the case. Messer Raffaello did not grant a postponement; a week later, on 6 and 7 August, the procurators were in court with their rebuttals to the latest affidavits of their opponent. The vicar general then instructed the procurators to bring their witnesses to the curia within two weeks.

Five witnesses called by Messer Stefano on Lusanna's behalf assembled on 16 August in the church of San Salvatore to take the oath before the vicar general. That evening Ser Piero Migliorelli appeared with his corps of seventeen witnesses, all of whom swore to tell the truth in their testimony. The judge allowed each procurator three days to submit to him their instructions for the interrogation of the witnesses. Before submitting his *interrogativa* to the court, Ser Piero made a final effort to stop the process. He petitioned the vicar general to absolve his client Giovanni of the charges brought by Lusanna and to order her "to observe perpetual silence" on the case and pay the court costs. The vicar general ordered Lusanna's procurator to respond to this petition on the next day, but Messer Stefano's rebuttal was not recorded in the protocol. Messer Raffaello did not really need his legal rejoinder to decide that the process should continue.

The procurators scrutinized each *capitolo* of their opponent's argument, probing for weaknesses. In suggesting questions that should be addressed to their adversary's witnesses, they sought to elicit information that would strengthen their own case and cast doubts on the behavior, motives, and reputations of those testifying for the opposition. Thus, Ser Piero focused on the marriage that had allegedly been celebrated between Giovanni and Lusanna in May 1453. The witnesses who claimed under oath to have been present should be asked about the particular events of that day. Since Giovanni insisted that the ceremony had never taken place, Ser Piero hoped to show, through contradictions in the testimony, that the account of the ceremony was a fabrication. Who was present in Antonio's house on that day? What did the bride and groom wear? What words were spoken during the ceremony? What was served at the wedding feast? Was there any discussion concerning a dowry and its amount? Relying upon his knowledge of Florentine marriage customs, Ser Piero wished to know "in what manner the marriage was consummated; who undressed Lusanna; whether a florin was placed in the bed; what was the name of the servant; whether Lusanna and Giovanni drank or ate in bed; how many eggs Lusanna drank; at what time Giovanni left the house."

Lusanna's procurator, Messer Stefano, reminded the vicar general of his responsibility to warn each witness who testified for Giovanni of the importance of the oath "and the grave danger to body and soul for false testimony." They should be informed that a copy of their evidence would be redacted and publicized and that they could be prosecuted in a secular court for lying under oath. Messer Stefano was particularly interested in clarifying the relationship between Giovanni and his witnesses. The judge should ascertain whether they owed money to him and whether they were his business associates or godparents or bound to him by ties of "friendship, brotherhood, or association." Were any of the

witnesses bribed to accuse Lusanna before the *podestà*'s court of poisoning her husband Andrea?
Finally, the witnesses should be asked whether
they had received, or hoped to receive, any
money or gift to testify in this process.

On 20 August, the day after this affidavit was
submitted to the court, the vicar general began his
questioning of the witnesses. The first phase of
that interrogation, involving fifteen witnesses,
was completed on 2 September. On that day, Ser
Domenico da Figline, perhaps sensing that his
case was weak, summoned five additional witnesses to testify on Giovanni's behalf. Not to be
outdone by his opponent, Messer Stefano then
produced a supplementary list of seven witnesses, all from the *pieve* of Pitiana, to give evidence concerning Lusanna's summer idyll with
Giovanni. As each new group of witnesses was
presented to the court, the opposing counsel was
entitled to submit a list of questions to be addressed to them. The last witnesses called by both
sides appeared in court on 11 September; two had
been summoned by Giovanni's procurator, five
by Lusanna's. Only the testimony of Giovanni's
final witnesses is recorded in Ser Filippo Mazzei's
protocol. By mid-September the testimonial
phase of the process had ended.

On 27 September, two weeks after the last
witnesses had been questioned, Messer Stefano
asked that the record of the testimony be made
available to the procurators so that they would
have the opportunity to challenge the witnesses
and their depositions. Accepting this request,

Messer Raffaello set a deadline for the procurators
to respond formally to the evidence presented by
opposing witnesses. Ser Piero Migliorelli presented his objections on 22 October. The witnesses who testified for Lusanna were people of
low status and reputation, whose evidence was
discredited by the fact that they were bound to her
by ties of blood or friendship. The testimony of
Cosa, Mea, and Antonio should be ignored, he
argued, while that of the peasants from Pitiana
was equally suspect since they were her friends
and Giovanni's enemies. Fra Felice Asini's testimony was not credible for another reason. Two
years before, "in the city of Cortona, he was pun-
ished by the captain for his crimes . . . as an in-
famous friar and malefactor." For his misdeeds,
which were not specified, he was escorted to the
main square of Cortona and there exposed to
public view with his head shaven and his gown
ripped in the rear. Lusanna's witnesses had per-
jured themselves, Ser Piero insisted, particularly
"when they said that a marriage had been contracted between Giovanni and Lusanna in the
month of May [1453]." According to the procurator's affidavit, Giovanni had been in Siena during that month and could not have participated in
a marriage ceremony in Florence.

Even more censorious were the charges made
by Lusanna's procurator, Messer Stefano, against
Giovanni della Casa's witnesses. They had all
conspired to defame his client; they were, moreover, "perjurers, vagabonds, paupers, loiterers in
taverns, gamblers, drunks, pimps, blasphemers

against God and the saints, [people] of bad reputation and frivolous opinions." Unless subjected
to torture, they could not be believed, and their
evidence was wholly without value. Messer Stefano claimed to find discrepancies and contradictions in their testimony; he was particularly critical of those witnesses who had described the
meetings between Giovanni and Lusanna in the
homes of Piero Cavicciuli and Niccolò Magaldi.
No credence could be given, for example, to the
testimony of those who asserted that they had
seen the lovers lying together on a bed because
even prostitutes in brothels closed the door of the
room when they entertained a client. If the evidence concerning these assignations were true,
which Messer Stefano denied, then Piero Cavicciuli and Niccolò Magaldi were guilty of abetting
an adulterous relationship. Niccolò and his wife
and sons were known to be Lusanna's enemies because they had testified falsely against her in the
podestà's court. Their testimony was manifestly
false since the Signoria and the colleges had
quashed the charges against his client.

With the ventilation of these charges and
countercharges by the opposing procurators, the
case of Lusanna and Giovanni was moving inex-
orably toward its conclusion. In the final stages
of the trial, Giovanni's procurators betrayed by
their tactics some anxiety over the outcome. On
27 October Ser Domenico presented an affidavit
to the court charging that Messer Stefano of
Prato had been excommunicated two years before by the auditor of the Apostolic Camera in

In the bridal chamber

Rome, a claim that Messer Stefano asserted to be false. On the same day Lusanna's brother Antonio appeared as her procurator and asked that a decision in the case be pronounced by the vicar general. Ser Domenico made one final attempt to delay the proceedings by charging that Antonio had also been excommunicated by the bishop of Fiesole for having assaulted his brother, the priest Marco. After Antonio denied this accusation, the vicar general expressed his annoyance over the legal maneuvers by leaving his bench and announcing that he would do nothing further that evening about the case.

Undeterred by the judge's displeasure, Giovanni's procurators pursued their strategy of procrastination. On 29 October Ser Piero and his colleague Ser Domenico informed the vicar general that they had been relieved of their responsibilities as the legal representatives of their client; they offered to submit to the court a document attesting to the revocation of their procuratorial authority. Lusanna's procurator argued that the affidavit should not be accepted. The vicar general ruled that the revocation of the procurations had occurred after the testimony of witnesses had been heard and, in any event, was not germane to the resolution of the case. He ordered Giovanni's procurators to bring their client to the archiepiscopal palace that evening to hear him pronounce the sentence. In a final, desperate move to postpone the judgment, three distinguished lawyers—Messer Zanobi Guasconi, Messer Piero di Jacopo Ambrosini, and Messer Benedetto Ac-

colti—arose in court to identify themselves as ad-
vocates for Giovanni della Casa. They petitioned
the vicar general to state publicly "whether he
had any doubts concerning the case, the witnesses, and their testimony." If he had no doubts,
then they requested a delay to allow them to present legal arguments that would support Giovanni's cause and demonstrate "the iniquity and in-
justice" of Lusanna's complaint.

In a statement that barely concealed his anger,
Messer Raffaello denied the lawyers' petition. He
reaffirmed his determination to pronounce his
decision later that day and refused to hear additional arguments "since he had already heard
them on several occasions and had their written
affidavits." Supporting his decision was the advice of a learned doctor of law, Messer Mariano
Sozzini. Stung by the suggestion that their action
might be construed as unprofessional, the lawyers insisted that they had never made any statements, orally or in writing, concerning the mer-
its of the case, "nor were they accustomed to
prolonging any process but were motivated
solely by the interests of their clients, by their
honor, and that of the court." They again appealed to the judge to give them more time to
present their arguments, "since the time is too
short and the case too arduous, and they have always acted honestly in every cause." Neither that
appeal nor a last-minute protest submitted to him
in the late afternoon by Giovanni's brother Jacopo
made any impression upon Messer Raffaello. He
labeled Jacopo's petition as "frivolous and with-

out merit" and proceeded to read the court's decision.

The session at which the sentence was read by the vicar general in the name of Archbishop Antoninus was attended by a large crowd of clergy and laymen (*clericis et laiciis in multitudine copiosa*), which included as formal witnesses two doctors of decretals, two cathedral canons, the rector of the hospital of San Paolo, and the proconsul of the guild of judges and notaries. Lusanna was represented by a new procurator, Ser Niccolò Francesci, but neither Giovanni della Casa nor his procurators were present, though they had been instructed to appear. The sentence began, "In the name of God, amen. We, friar Antoninus, O.P., . . . archbishop of Florence and . . . judge and commissioner of this case specially delegated by Pope Calixtus III, authorized to investigate and to decide the matrimonial case between the parties identified below." The text of the judgment contained a copy of the pope's letter to Antoninus that had initiated the process; it listed each step of the process: the presentations, the challenges, the testimony, the rebuttals. "We decree [the sentence concluded] . . . that a valid marriage between Lusanna and Giovanni . . . was contracted according to the form of the law and the sacred canons." Consequently, the second marriage between Giovanni and Marietta Rucellai was nullified since it violated the canons and the rites of the Holy Roman Church. Giovanni was ordered to acknowledge Lusanna publicly as his lawful wife and to treat her "with marital affection," under penalty of excommunication. For having violated the canon law by his second marriage, he was fined a total of 1,400 florins: 100 florins to the archiepiscopal curia for alms to the poor, 1,000 florins to the communal office responsible for the grain supply, and 300 florins to the Apostolic Camera "to be spent on ships against the Turks, enemies of the Christian faith." Giovanni was also assessed the court costs in the lengthy judicial process.

In promulgating their decision in this case, Archbishop Antoninus and his vicar general were meticulous in following the prescribed legal forms; they cited the papal *breve* that authorized their investigation of Lusanna's complaint and noted each stage in the lengthy and litigious process. But they provided no clues to their assessment of the evidence or to the interpretation of canon law that produced their judgment in favor of Lusanna. Antoninus's knowledge of the canon law concerning marriage was solid and thorough, as is attested by the chapters devoted to the subject in his *Summa*. Both he and his vicar general had extensive experience in church courts and, it must be assumed, in judging marriage cases comparable to that of Lusanna and Giovanni. They knew the law and could seek guidance in the opinions of the jurisconsults who had written about marriage. But a just disposition of the case depended heavily upon their assessment of the facts. Whose version of events and the relationship between Giovanni and Lusanna should be believed?

In his *Summa* Antoninus wrote extensively about the proper administration of justice and the specific problems that confronted a judge, whether ecclesiastical or secular, in attempting to fulfill his responsibilities. Judges, he wrote, should be knowledgeable, diligent, and fair; they should be as concerned for the rights of the poor and the lowly as for those of the rich and the powerful. Magistrates were continually tempted to deviate from this principle, as one witness in this case, Giuliano Gondi, candidly admitted. "As mutual friends are accustomed to do for each other," he testified, he had interceded with the present *podestà* on behalf of Giovanni della Casa when he was jailed for failing to pay his taxes. That mistakes were inevitable in judging cases Antoninus readily conceded, since the judicial decision "is based on the information provided by others." In interrogating witnesses and evaluating their testimony, the judge should consider the status of each and the plausibility of their statements. Relatives and friends of the principals were not ideal witnesses; their testimony was inevitably suspect. The judge should seek to reconcile all the evidence submitted in a case. If discrepancies on major points existed, then "the testimony of the greater number [of witnesses] should prevail, unless for the opposing side the worthiness of the individuals is such that it overwhelms the weight of numbers."

In their examination of the witnesses called by the procurators for Lusanna and Giovanni, the archbishop and his vicar general followed carefully the prescribed procedures, interrogating every witness on each chapter of the affidavit submitted by the procurator for their side. Thus, Ser Filippo read to Cosa, Lusanna's sister-in-law, a vernacular translation of the assertions made by Messer Stefano of Prato. How long and in what context had she known Lusanna? Where had the widow Lusanna lived after Andrea's death? In what circumstances did Giovanni della Casa enter Antonio's house to discuss marriage with Lusanna? What occurred, who was present, and what was said on that day in May 1453 when, according to Lusanna's procurator, she and Giovanni were married? What was the nature of their relationship after the ceremony? How often did Giovanni visit Lusanna; how did he treat her? What clothing did she wear in the house and outside? The judges did not limit themselves to the arguments advanced on Lusanna's behalf; they also asked Cosa if she had any knowledge of relations between Giovanni and Lusanna before Andrea's death and, specifically, of those meetings described by Giovanni's witnesses, in the homes of his employees Piero Cavicciuli and Niccolò Magaldi. Concerning these meetings and any sexual relations between Lusanna and Giovanni prior to the spring of 1453, Cosa stated that she knew nothing.

Each witness called by Lusanna's procurators was questioned exhaustively by the judges and Ser Filippo, as were those summoned to testify on Giovanni's behalf. How long and in what context had they known the principals in the case?

A domestic scene

What details could they remember of the relations between the lovers and, specifically, the occasions when Giovanni, at Lusanna's instigation,
promised to marry her if her husband died? Had
they witnessed or heard about the alleged wedding ceremony in May 1453? Had Giovanni, in
their presence, ever alluded to Lusanna as his
wife? What did they know and what had they
heard about the condition and reputation of the
couple? The judges prodded memories about
facts and sought opinions about behavior and
reputations. What did the witnesses know and
what had they heard about Giovanni's wealth and
social rank and that of his family? Where did Lusanna, her father, and her first husband fit into
Florence's social order?

By this exhaustive interrogation the judges
searched for clues to the credibility of the witnesses that would enable them to establish the
facts in the case and evaluate the statements about
public opinion (*publica vox et fama*). Much of the
testimony for Lusanna's case came from her close
relatives, who clearly had a vested interest in depicting her as a virtuous woman betrayed by her
husband. How reliable was the evidence of the
one apparently independent witness, Fra Felice
Asini, whose character had been blackened by
Giovanni's procurator? The critical testimony for
Giovanni's case was given by neighbors of Lusanna who had been on intimate terms with her
and her family and had then become hostile witnesses. How could their *volte-face* be explained?
Were they, and particularly the women, resentful

of Lusanna's aspirations to marry a wealthy and socially prominent man? Were Piero Cavicciuli and Niccolò Magaldi induced to testify for Giovanni by the fact that he had once been their employer and was the godfather of their children? Had they been bribed? Giuliana Magaldi had testified that Lusanna's brother Antonio had offered her 200 florins if she, her husband, and her son "would testify that they had seen—and were present when—Giovanni della Casa contracted a marriage with Lusanna." Had this attempt at bribery actually occurred, or was Giuliana describing a conversation with Giovanni della Casa?

That attempts were often, perhaps routinely, made to suborn witnesses is suggested by the testimony in a case heard in the episcopal court of Feltre in 1545–47. Giovanni Andrea Dalla Croce and his sister Fiorenza claimed that she was legally married to Gerolamo de Mezzan. But Gerolamo denied that he had ever promised to marry Fiorenza. According to the sworn testimony of several witnesses, he had appealed to them "to save his honor and his property" by corroborating his story. One witness stated that Gerolamo had threatened to charge her with perjury and "shame your family" if she testified against him. In appealing to a notary named Ser Vittore to intercede on his behalf with a witness named Bortolota, Gerolamo said, "We have always been friends and, indeed, we are distantly related (*semo un poco parenti*)." Monna Fiorenza and her brother Andrea employed similar tactics in conversations with witnesses. To a peasant woman named Bianca, Fiorenza allegedly said, "If you have to lie to help me, it will not be a sin, because it is better to help a woman of my condition instead of a man. Unlike a woman, a man can go anywhere in the world." Bianca, however, refused to perjure herself, insisting that she would not receive absolution for that sin. When Fiorenza told her that a friar of her acquaintance would absolve her, Bianca retorted, "I don't want to see any friar; I want to go to my confessor, Father Simone, as long as he lives!"

Of crucial importance for Giovanni's case were the accounts of the lovers' meetings in the homes of Piero Cavicciuli and Niccolò Magaldi. If the judges were to accept the testimony of the six witnesses who claimed to be present at those assignations, then Lusanna's assertion that she had had no relations with Giovanni before her first husband's death was patently false. The centerpiece for her case was, of course, the marriage ceremony attended by Antonio, Mea, Cosa, and Fra Felice Asini. These witnesses also asserted that Niccolò Magaldi, his wife, and children were present at the ceremony and that Niccolò and his son Antonio had gone to Santa Croce to fetch the friar. Niccolò Magaldi, however, denied those assertions: he had never eaten a meal in the house of Lusanna's brother Antonio; he had never spoken to Fra Felice Asini. His wife, Giuliana, and son Andrea also testified that they had not been present at the ceremony, nor had they dined in Antonio's house. From this testimony, the judges could only conclude that some witnesses were guilty of perjury.

Indeed, one witness for Giovanni, Giuliana Magaldi, confessed that she had lied in her testimony to the court. On 29 September, in the church of San Salvatore in the presence of Antoninus and his chaplain, Giuliana stated under oath that only one part of her testimony in the case was accurate. While Giovanni was in her house, she had heard him say, "I have promised to take Lusanna for my wife if her husband should die." She added that "she had not seen nor heard anything else . . . and that whatever else she deposed is not true and so she revokes it." She thus withdrew her evidence concerning the couple's tryst in her bedroom, her nonattendance at their wedding ceremony, and her conversation with Lusanna about silver powder being placed in Andrea Nucci's food prior to his death.

From his decision it is evident that Antoninus accepted Lusanna's version of her relationship with Giovanni and, in particular, her denial that she had ever been unchaste. In the *Summa* he wrote that a marriage contracted between adulterers who had vowed to marry was invalid if the promise was made while one of the partners had a living spouse. Antoninus described a case that paralleled exactly the situation described by Giovanni della Casa's procurator. If a certain Berta had extracted a promise from her partner in adultery that he would marry her if her husband died, that marriage was invalid. The office of the papal penitentiary in Rome was frequently requested to validate marriages contracted in such circumstances. In 1457 Ser Francesco Martini and his wife Lena, inhabitants of the Swiss diocese of Lucerne, confessed that they had committed adultery while both were married and had promised each other to marry if and when their spouses died. After they remarried, they had doubts about the validity of their union, which motivated them to seek a papal dispensation.

Antoninus thus concluded that an honest and virtuous widow had exchanged vows with, and received a ring from, Giovanni della Casa in the home of her brother Antonio, before a group of witnesses including the officiating friar. The essential requirement of a valid marriage, Antoninus wrote in his *Summa*, was the consent of both parties. Had the archbishop been persuaded that Giovanni did not freely consent to the union, he would have been bound to declare the marriage invalid. This marriage could be described as clandestine, since it was not publicized. Antoninus did not approve of marriages contracted without witnesses and without bans, but he did permit exceptions to the general prohibition against secret marriages. In some places (for example, Florence) it was not customary to publish bans; instead, the parish priest or a notary publicized the betrothal (*sponsalia*) of the parties, which could be announced in front of a church or in a private home. In other circumstances Antoninus was prepared to forego the publication of bans. These cases involved unions that were exceptional, even abnormal, such as those between rich and poor, young and old, noble and ignoble, where publicity might bring humiliation to the couple. These conditions all applied in some degree to the marriage of Giovanni and Lusanna, as did the justification for secrecy when relatives were likely to oppose the union.

Antoninus's judgment in Lusanna's favor was based on his interpretation of the evidence in the case; it also reflected his sense of his pastoral mission as "father of poor and miserable persons." He may have seen Lusanna, a widow from a modest social background similar to his own, as a victim of those powerful members of Florence's ruling elite with whom he had quarreled on several occasions and whose ruthless tactics were quite familiar to him. Giovanni della Casa was a rich banker and moneylender, possibly guilty of usury (see below, chapter 5). Antoninus's hostility to such men was so well known in Florence that, on one occasion, the Signoria asked its ambassador in Rome to arrange for the transfer of a usury case from Antoninus's court to the curia, "because they [the defendants] can hope to find better justice there." Antoninus may also have been persuaded that Giovanni della Casa had suborned witnesses, inducing them to testify falsely on his behalf. He would have understood how a poor woman like Giuliana Magaldi could be tempted by a bribe yet ultimately so frightened by her perjury that she recanted her testimony. The archbishop arrived at a decision that was

74

consonant with his knowledge of the law, his view of his pastoral role, and his social perceptions. Later, in Rome, other ecclesiastical judges would apply similar kinds of criteria to arrive at a different decision about the case.

LOVE, MARRIAGE,
AND THE
SOCIAL ORDER

Ut solent amatores: "as lovers are wont to do." This phrase, repeated several times in the testimony given at the process, suggests that witnesses who observed the relationship between Giovanni and Lusanna could fit their impressions into recognizable patterns. They noted Giovanni's promenades in front of Lusanna's house, his pursuit when she walked to church, their exchange of amorous glances, their intimate conversations. Such behavior in public and private places, between rich and poor, married and unmarried, secular and clerical, was familiar enough to be portrayed in *novelle*, popular poems, and songs. The pursuit of women was a common pastime of young Florentine males of all classes, but particularly among the rich and wellborn. The community naturally sought to control these encounters by defining limits and imposing penalties upon transgressors. Such restraints functioned most effectively upon upper-class women, whether nubile, married, or widowed. So important was the ideal of feminine chastity to family

honor that it was guarded as jealously by male
relatives as was their property. A stain upon a
family's reputation adversely affected its social
standing and, specifically, its ability to contract
good marriages for its daughters. Such consid-
erations explain the anger expressed in 1383 by
Paolo Sassetti when describing the death of his
cousin Letta, the concubine of Giovanni Porcel-
lini: "May the devil take her soul for she has
brought shame and dishonor to our family."

That Giovanni and Lusanna had been lovers
for many years before and after her husband's
death would seem to be beyond dispute. So many
witnesses had seen them in compromising situa-
tions and so widespread were neighborhood rumors about their affair that Lusanna's assertion
that she was a chaste woman must be discounted.
The affair began in the 1440s when both were in
their twenties and after Lusanna had been married
for five years. The opportunities for their meetings were infrequent, since both had domestic
obligations and Giovanni was often absent from
Florence on business. Young men of his age and
background did not normally marry until their
mid-thirties; they commonly sought sexual partners from among their social inferiors: servants,
peasant girls, poor widows, and—occasionally—
married women. Hundreds of illegitimate children, the product of such liaisons, are identified
in *catasto* volumes and the records of the city's
foundling homes. In his 1458 declaration Giovanni listed his two illegitimate sons, Carlo and

Marco (born in 1453 and 1455), and also his father's bastard child, Girolamo (born in 1452).

The most remarkable feature of the relationship between Giovanni and Lusanna was its lon-
gevity; it continued for twelve years, from 1443
to 1455. If his initial infatuation had been motivated by physical attraction and sexual desire,
Giovanni's feelings for Lusanna apparently deep-
ened over time. There was clearly some truth in
her statement to Monna Fiora that "Giovanni is
passionately in love with me." While they coha-
bited in her brother's house after their marriage,
Giovanni gave her valuable gifts and the services
of the slave Caterina, a rare phenomenon in artisan households. Concerned for Lusanna's reputation, he endeavored to keep their relationship a
secret in the city, though to acquaintances like
Giuliano Gondi, Carlo Guasconi, Cipriano Nuti,
and Matteo Augustini he confided that Lusanna
was his mistress. Even after his marriage to Marietta Rucellai he visited Lusanna, discussed her
future, and sought to arrange a marriage for her.
But neither during their affair nor after its termi-
nation did he experience any feelings of guilt or
remorse for his behavior. Though adultery was a
violation of both secular and canon law, Giovanni's procurator candidly admitted in a church
court that his client had sexual relations with Lusanna while she was married to Andrea. Obviously, Giovanni did not fear prosecution for his
offense, which was so prevalent and widely tol-
erated that it was rarely penalized by Florentine

courts. Only poor wretches like Tommasa, wife of Antonio di Berto, and her lover, Nanni di Romolo, "of base condition and reputation," were convicted of adultery in Florence's secular tribunals; privileged citizens like Andrea di Niccolò Rucellai could maintain a concubine for twenty years, immune from legal sanctions and social opprobrium. Giovanni della Casa would have incurred censure only if he had seduced an unmarried girl from a respectable family or had violated a nun. But even such peccadillos could be forgiven, as was Fra Filippo Lippi's seduction of Lucrezia Buti, a cloistered nun from a convent in Prato.

Giovanni's behavior thus conformed in most respects to the conventions of his sex, age, and class. In his twenties, while establishing himself in the business world and before contemplating marriage, he began an affair with a beautiful woman, the daughter and wife of an artisan. His promise to marry Lusanna if she were to become a widow was doubtless made to placate her and insure that their liaison would continue. But how to explain his participation in a nuptial ceremony that involved an exchange of vows and rings? Was his love for Lusanna at that moment so intense that he truly desired her as his wife? Or did he believe that a clandestine ceremony, unrecorded by a notary, was invalid and that he was participating in a charade? Such a conclusion was possible, given the ambiguities of marriage law and practice in pre-Tridentine Europe.

Florentine marriages were typically public

A wedding scene

and ritualized affairs, the product of lengthy and arduous negotiations between relatives and friends of the families and often abetted by professional matchmakers. A preliminary and private agreement between the parties was symbolized by an exchange of handshakes (*impalmamento*). This was followed by a public meeting—in effect, a betrothal ceremony (*sponsalia*)—of male relatives from both families, normally held in a church, in which the groom and the bride's father or guardian accepted the terms of the marriage contract as redacted by a notary. The breach of this contract was a very serious matter that could lead to lawsuits and even vendettas. Subsequent to the formal betrothal the bride and groom, each accompanied by kinfolk and friends, met in the girl's house, where in response to the notary's questions they exchanged vows and rings and participated in a wedding banquet. Like the *sponsalia*, the solemnization of the union was recorded by the notary and copied in his register. Then the bride and her entourage made a formal and festive journey through the city streets to her husband's house, where the physical consummation of the marriage occurred. It is noteworthy that the Florentine clergy were not formal participants in any phase of this complex ritual of betrothal and marriage.

Though inconclusive, the evidence suggests that Giovanni did accept the legality of his clandestine marriage with Lusanna. But after his father's death in February 1455, he made no effort to publicize his matrimony. If he had scruples about the validity of the 1453 ceremony, he, like others in his predicament, could have obtained a ruling from the Holy Penitentiary that his marriage to Lusanna was licit. Instead, he went to Rome not to legalize his bond but to dissolve it. Unsuccessful in his efforts to obtain an annulment, he decided to ignore his marital status and arrange for a union with Marietta Rucellai. As late as 1453 Giovanni, the younger son, could still play the role of a feckless bachelor who was unwilling to assume family responsibilities. Then in 1454 his brother Antonio died leaving a widow and three small children. The death of his father a year later may finally have persuaded him that a conventional marriage to a girl of "noble" lineage who would bring him a sizeable dowry was essential to his family's welfare and reputation.

Lusanna was an extraordinary woman, who does not fit neatly into any of the standard roles of chaste wives and widows or cloistered nuns that were defined for women of her time and social rank. She was obviously a woman of strong passions, who found little satisfaction in her marriage and was prepared to risk dishonor to follow the dictates of her heart. On at least two occasions she took the initiative in arranging for trysts with Giovanni. If the testimony of Giovanni Panciatichi and Niccolò Magaldi can be believed, she had sexual relations with men besides Giovanni della Casa. Rumors of her liaison with one man had reached Monna Fiora, who stated in her testimony that she had chided Lusanna for her promiscuous behavior. Lusanna explained to her that she had always loved Giovanni more than his rival but that he had gone away and "now that he has returned, I love him as much as I did before, and I don't wish to have anything to do with [the other man]." Both Niccolò Magaldi and his wife, Giuliana, testified that horns (*cornia bestiarum*) had been nailed over the lintel of Lusanna's house and that her husband, Andrea, had been called a cuckold (*becco*) by one of his wife's lovers "from the doorway of his house to the Canto della Paglia, in sight of the entire neighborhood." Was Andrea's apparent indifference to his wife's behavior and reputation due to his particular sexual orientation? Lusanna's situation may have been similar to that of a distraught young wife, Alessandra de' Bardi, who accused her husband, Raphaele Acciaiuoli, of spurning her (*spernendo dictam suam uxorem et raro cum ea dormiendo*) and engaging in acts of sodomy.

Vain and seductive in her demeanor, so her neighbors described Lusanna, a married woman who had one lover and possibly several. Her barren state may have induced her to find satisfaction in illicit relations, perhaps even to hope that she might conceive a child. Monna Fiora, the wife of Angelo di Francesco dell'Opere, reported a conversation with Lusanna which, if true, throws some light upon her personality and mental state. In 1451 Fiora had visited the home of Lusanna's stepmother, Mea, and there she met Lusanna, who told her that she was pregnant. Fiora responded, "You can't be pregnant, because you have been married for several years without bearing children." She added, "Let me touch your belly so that I can determine whether you are pregnant." A mortified Lusanna confessed that she had lied to Fiora, and she cried, "How can I have a baby?" Fiora told her that she was acquainted with a pregnant slave girl who would be willing to give her infant to Lusanna. Lusanna vetoed this proposal, saying that "Giovanni della Casa is in love with me, and his relatives would think that the child was his." Continuing her testimony, Fiora reported her visit to a wet nurse named Santa, who fed foundlings for one of the city's orphanages. Santa refused to be involved in any scheme to find a baby for Lusanna. It was a capital offense, she said, and she added, "You know what will happen with this business; someone will lose his head." Fiora told Lusanna's sister-in-law Cosa, "I do not wish to be involved in this affair because the penalty is death (*però chè ella è pena capitale*)."

Giovanni's procurators stressed Lusanna's barren state in arguing that he would never have considered marriage with her. Her legal representatives denied the allegation, insisting that she was the mother of a boy named Francesco, "who now lives, walks, eats, and talks." But that child was not seen by any witness and seems to have been as fictitious as the pregnancy described by Monna Fiora. The contradictions in the testimony concerning Lusanna's maternity suggest that rumors heard on Florentine streets were not wholly reliable sources of information and that neighbors were not always privy to each other's

A conversation by the fire

domestic lives. Monna Tita reported that she had been told that Lusanna was nursing her child but then was not allowed to inspect her breasts. Giovanni Panciatichi and Andrea di Niccolò Magaldi, who had worked for Lusanna's first husband, testified that they had heard different stories about Lusanna: that she had, and had not, given birth to a child. Andrea Magaldi also reported a bizarre conversation with his mother, Giuliana, who allegedly had been informed by the ubiquitous Fra Felice Asini that Lusanna had indeed become a mother. According to Andrea's testimony, the friar had advised Lusanna to train the boy for the clergy so that he would not inherit a full share of his father's estate.

Lusanna's reputation was a critical issue in this case, and the testimony of her neighbors provides a rare glimpse of the moral values of Florence's artisan community. Witnesses called by Giovanni della Casa expressed the judgment that she was a *mala femina* who had violated her marriage vow and dishonored herself, her husband, and her family. The fastening of horns over the doorway was a common practice in Mediterranean communities to indicate that a social norm had been violated and to warn the victims to mend their ways. These criticisms notwithstanding, none of Lusanna's neighbors described her as a prostitute, nor were they so scandalized by her behavior that they refused to associate with her. Monna Tita and Monna Fiora frequently visited Lusanna and her stepmother, offering advice on her relationship with Giovanni. The most concrete evidence

that Lusanna had retained some measure of respectability was the competition for her hand by
several suitors after Andrea's death. Marriage
brokers approached her and her brother Antonio,
presenting lists of prospective husbands for ap-
proval. Had Lusanna decided to give up Giovanni, she could have espoused a man of her own
rank or even someone like Piero Cecchi, who was
marginally higher on the social scale. But she was
determined to force Giovanni to honor his promise and accept the legitimacy of their marital
bond.

Though Lusanna's reputation was not im-
maculate, she was not perceived as a fallen
woman or shunned as a pariah by her neighbors.
By wearing widow's garb and avoiding any public contact with Giovanni, she sought to project
an image of matronly respectability. With her
dowry of 250 florins and her family connections,
she was not as vulnerable as many Florentine
widows, who were dependent on charity, lived
as tertiaries (*pinzochere*) or pensioners in religious houses, or were forced to work as servants
(and sometimes concubines) in the households of
merchants and priests. While the moral code defined in sermons and in civic legislation did apply
to women like Lusanna, it may have been atten-
uated or less rigidly enforced by the particular circumstances of her condition. Women from the
artisanal class enjoyed a greater degree of social
freedom than did their chaperoned, aristocratic
sisters. They could move freely in the streets,
gossip with neighbors, shop in the markets, at-

tend services in their local church. Some worked in their husbands' *botteghe* or, if widowed, as independent shopkeepers or spinners and weavers in the city's cloth industry. But the evidence is too sparse to permit any firm conclusions concerning the sexual mores of these women or to determine whether Lusanna's behavior was exceptional.

From this ambiguous, even contradictory, evidence, what image of Lusanna's personality can be constructed? The leitmotiv of her adult life was her love for Giovanni della Casa. So strong was her passion that she was willing to flout the moral code of her society and risk the loss of honor and reputation. Her efforts to induce her lover to marry her were motivated by her emotions and her craving for respectability and, perhaps, by a yearning for higher social rank. Though she may have been sexually promiscuous in the early years of her marriage with Andrea, she was apparently faithful to Giovanni after their wedding in 1453. She lived for the moment when Giovanni would acknowledge her publicly as his wife. When, after his father's death, he failed to honor his commitment, she was initially uncertain about her status and future. Though the evidence on this point is inconclusive, she may even have considered the dissolution of her bond with Giovanni. So the marriage broker Mazza del Mazza testified when he recalled a conversation with Lusanna in May 1455. Responding to his query about her plans, she said, "I am expecting an absolution from the pope, since Giovanni della Casa has given me a ring and he has told me that a papal absolution should arrive so that we can both remarry. But the absolution hasn't come, so don't involve yourself further in this affair." But once she realized what she would lose emotionally and socially by this stratagem, Lusanna decided to fight for her rights and her honor. "That traitor Giovanni has deceived me," she exclaimed to Monna Fiora; "I am his wife and he has taken the daughter of Piero di Cardinale [Rucellai], and he has also given me a ring!"

The inconsistencies in Lusanna's character are more easily described than explained. She was at times aggressive, willful, and manipulative; at other times, docile and passive. In her relationship with Giovanni, she played the role, first, of seductive temptress, then, the cajoling mistress, and finally, the betrayed and vengeful wife. Since her affair with Giovanni began, Lusanna was forced to hide her true feelings and desires from kinfolk and neighbors. Living in this shadowy world of deception and dissimulation undoubtedly left its mark upon her personality. She may have circulated rumors of giving birth to, and rearing, children as a form of wish fulfillment and to refute allegations that she was sterile. She appeared to believe that Giovanni's promise of marriage gave her license to have sexual relations with her lover. When Giuliana Magaldi criticized her for sleeping with Giovanni in her house, Lusanna replied, "I did not come here to commit wrong, but for a good purpose," which she defined as persuading Giovanni to renew his promise of marriage. The argument did not convince Giuliana, who told her with some exaggeration, "I will have you burned because you have two husbands!" Lusanna's "tangled web" of deception was most dramatically revealed in the testimony of her neighbor Monna Fiora, who had asked about her exchange of wedding rings with Giovanni. Irritated by Lusanna's contradictory statements, Fiora cried, "Oh, you liar! You tell me nothing but falsehoods! You said that you received the ring in the house of Monna Giuliana [Magaldi], and now Monna Mea says that you received it here. . . . I do not believe either of you!"

Lusanna's story describes one woman's struggle to gain a measure of personal independence in a male-dominated world. In Renaissance Florence and in Europe generally, the sentiment of love and the institution of marriage were rarely combined into the felicitous state that later became the Western ideal, if not often the reality. Lusanna was exceptional in her determination to transform an affective bond into a legal covenant. By inducing Giovanni to articulate his promise of marriage before witnesses, she sought guarantees for her future. The allegations that she poisoned her husband are scarcely credible; Andrea apparently died of catarrh. But some Florentine women did take such extreme measures to escape from their marriages; their pathetic stories and their fate are described in the records of the criminal courts. Lusanna accepted Giovanni's argument in favor of an unnotarized, clandestine marriage, believing that their exchange of rings before witnesses and their cohabitation would be sufficient to legalize the matrimony. During the difficult months when Giovanni was seeking to disengage himself from that bond, Lusanna assumed full responsibility for her life. She rejected the suitors that were proposed by marriage brokers; through her agent Monna Fiora, she inquired about the availability of Baldinaccio, who had attracted her interest. She enlisted the support of her female neighbors to persuade Giovanni to recognize their marriage. Finally, she persuaded her brother Antonio to take her case to the archbishop's court since women could only be represented by their legal guardians.

The relationship between Giovanni and Lusanna bridged two different milieux; its denouement in the archiepiscopal court provides a rare and revealing glimpse of social structures and values in Medicean Florence. Since it is richly documented, the upper-class world of Giovanni della Casa has been intensively explored; its salient features are well known. Membership in this community was determined primarily by the status of one's lineage. A legal brief submitted to the archiepiscopal court in 1480 on behalf of Benedetto di Roberto de' Rossi stated "that for three hundred years and longer in the city of Florence, there has existed a most distinguished, ancient, and noble family called Rossi, to which have belonged a great number of very honorable men and knights . . . and also doctors of both laws [civil and canon] who have possessed numerous castles and lands and have enjoyed the rights of

patronage to benefices in the city and diocese of
Florence, Volterra, and Arezzo." While no specific mention of wealth is made in this deposition,
it was an important criterion of high social rank.
So, too, was a family's political status, as mea-
sured by the important civic offices held by its
members. The witnesses called by Giovanni della
Casa cited all these qualities in their testimony.
According to Carlo Guasconi and Giuliano
Gondi, the Della Casa were solidly established in
the upper level of Florentine society. Family
members had occupied the most exalted offices in
the republic. Giovanni and his brothers were
prominent merchants and bankers, with companies based in Florence, Rome, Naples, Geneva,
and London. Giovanni Panciatichi testified that
he had known Giovanni for eighteen years; "he
is [a man] of good reputation, highly esteemed
in the mercantile community." Cipriano Nuti
stated that Giovanni "is reputed to be rich and
that in his opinion he would choose his wife
among nobly born women." Michele Scarlattini
noted that Giovanni's brothers had contracted
marriages with such prominent lineages as the
Cavalcanti, Carducci, and Mancini.

The social world of Giovanni della Casa em-
braced his kinfolk, his neighbors in San Lorenzo
and adjacent districts, and his business associates
in Florence and abroad. Giovanni's *catasto* declaration, submitted jointly with his brother Jacopo
in 1458, provides some evidence of the scope of
his business affairs. At that time, Giovanni was in
London, where he may have gone to collect debts

owed to his deceased brother Antonio, who had
established companies in Rome, Venice, and Geneva. Giovanni and his brother were thus involved in a Europe-wide network of mercantile
activities, similar in scope though not in magni-
tude to the Medici commercial empire. In addition to foreign creditors, the two brothers owed
money to Giuliano Gondi (a witness for Giovanni), to Piero Ginori, a neighbor from San Lorenzo, and to a dyer, Luca di Lorenzo. Among
their debtors were Florentine merchants (Piero
Corsi, Piero Guasconi, Jacopo Inghirami), the
tenant (*mezzadro*) who cultivated their land in the
Mugello, and two cloth spinners, who may have
been employed by Giovanni in his silk-manufacturing enterprise.

Giovanni's key witnesses were all recruited
from the city's artisan community: the craftsmen,
retail merchants, and cloth workers (and their
wives) who formed a middling stratum between
the aristocracy and the *popolo minuto* at the lower
end of the social hierarchy. Piero Cavicciuli and
Niccolò Magaldi had been employed by Giovanni in his silk-manufacturing enterprise. This
tie of economic dependency may explain their
willingness, however grudging, to permit him to
meet Lusanna in their homes in compromising
circumstances. Yet another important bond, that
of godparentage, linked Giovanni and Piero Cavicciuli, whose four children had been held at the
baptismal font by his employer. Giovanni may
have been exceptional in developing intimate relations with his workers and their families. The

A market in Florence

mother of Piero Cavicciuli, Monna Guglielma, testified that Giovanni and Lusanna frequently ate meals with Piero's family. Giovanni brought wine and victuals, "since that household could not afford such delicacies, and it was not proper that they [Giovanni and Lusanna] should eat at the expense of Piero's poor family." When Giovanni accompanied Lusanna to her brother's villa near Pitiana, he mixed easily with the peasants of that rural community. He shared meals with Antonio's family and their guests and participated in a celebration of the birth of a neighbor's son. Antonio Tronchi testified that Giovanni and Lusanna drank wine with the men and women who were present at that festive occasion and then visited the mother, "as is the custom."

Except for special occasions, baptismal feasts, or funerals, Florentine artisans and workers did not normally socialize with members of the city's aristocracy. Cosimo de' Medici did not invite bakers and weavers from his parish of San Lorenzo to dine with him in the family palace on the Via Larga. Within the city's neighborhoods, which might be based on a parish church, a street, or a piazza, artisans developed social networks among themselves. The bonds of friendship and mutual obligation were based on blood and marriage, on physical propinquity, on professional or work-related ties. The relationship between Lusanna's family and the Magaldi couple, Niccolò and Giuliana, had its origins in the late 1420s when Lusanna lived with her parents on the Via del Cocomero, adjacent to the house of Niccolò's married sister. Giuliana Magaldi testified that she had known Lusanna as an eight-year-old child. Reinforcing the social bonds between the families was the hiring by Lusanna's husband Andrea of a Magaldi boy as an apprentice in his linen shop. Piero and Tita Cavicciuli had been neighbors of Lusanna and Andrea on the Via San Gallo from the time of their marriage until Andrea's death in 1453. Monna Fiora, who testified against Lusanna, was the godmother of her brother Antonio. Lusanna did not call neighbors to testify on her behalf, relying instead upon close relatives (Antonio, Mea, Cosa) and dependents like the servant Ammannato, Fra Felice Asini, and the peasants from Pitiana. Either her neighborhood acquaintances were reluctant to appear as witnesses, or her procurators feared that their testimony might damage her cause.

The artisan world inhabited by Lusanna and her family was more constricted geographically and socially than was Giovanni's upper-class milieu. Witnesses described a broad range of contacts between the two societies, but their testimony suggests that marriages between aristocrats and artisans were violations of social conventions. Giuliano Gondi and Giovanni Panciatichi scoffed at the idea that Giovanni della Casa would ever have considered marriage with the daughter and widow of shopkeepers. But Lusanna's neighbors—artisans and their wives— were no more sympathetic to her aspirations. "You see now," Monna Fiora recalled her statement to Lusanna, "that what I told you is true; he

[Giovanni] will never take you as his wife." Even Lusanna's stepmother expressed her reservations about the marriage, "because Giovanni was so much wealthier than Antonio and Lusanna." The silk weaver Niccolò Magaldi and Monna Tita Cavicciuli, whose husband was a salaried employee of the Merchants' Court, both testified that the marriage was inappropriate because Giovanni's social status was so vastly superior to Lusanna's. Jealousy and resentment of Lusanna's social climbing may have influenced their views, but it is also clear that these people of middling condition accepted the notion of social hierarchy, and by its rules the daughters of artisans did not marry the sons of aristocratic families.

In presenting their case before the archbishop's court, Giovanni della Casa's procurators emphasized the height of the social barrier separating their client from his mistress. They contrasted his superior status with that of Lusanna's father, Benedetto, "a tailor of lowly condition and origins, not a Florentine but a native of Sclavonia, who married a servant girl from the Casentino." The tailor's profession was ranked among the inferior trades in Florence, and Lusanna could not have expected to marry a man of exalted rank. That claim was reaffirmed by Giovanni's upper-class witnesses—Giovanni Panciatichi, Giuliano Gondi, and Carlo Guasconi—who described as base and menial (*vile et mecanicum*) the professions of Lusanna's first husband, a linen-cloth maker, and his father, a baker. That distinction between mercantile and artisanal professions coincided with the division between Florence's greater and lesser guilds, or between guildsmen who did, and those who did not, work with their hands. Artisan witnesses were not willing to describe their trades in such derogatory terms, though Cipriano Nuti and Michele Scarlattini conceded that these métiers were not "noble" or comparable with the mercantile professions. Niccolò Magaldi described the linenmaker's trade as neither *nobile* nor *vile*, but rather *mediocre* or middling. He sought to distinguish between artisans, who belonged to a guild and who were independent entrepreneurs, and salaried laborers, who were excluded from guild membership. While accepting the social and occupational gulf between themselves and merchants of Giovanni della Casa's rank, these artisans insisted upon their place and their worthiness in Florence's professional hierarchy. When Cipriano Nuti was asked about the social condition of Lusanna's husband Andrea, whose father had been a baker, he responded, "There have been bakers who were members of the Signoria," the supreme magistracy of the Florentine republic.

The notion of a hierarchy of professions ranked according to "nobility" was a truism in this society, so universally accepted that it was rarely articulated. At the apex of the structure were the liberal professions (law, medicine, the humanities), whose practitioners held university degrees. Below them were the international merchants, then the retail shopkeepers and craftsmen, and at the bottom, the salaried laborers and

A Florentine cobbler

menials. Lusanna's procurator did not challenge this concept, but he did emphasize the dignity of artisanal activity, while questioning Giovanni della Casa's claim to professional respectability. He eulogized Lusanna's father, Benedetto, as a man who supported his family "with the labor of his hands and the sweat of his brow, who lived honorably and decently as a worthy Florentine guildsman." He did concede that some members of the Della Casa lineage were men of distinction who had occupied the highest offices of the state, but he argued that Giovanni's branch of the family was not of that quality. His grandfather Francesco, alias Baccello, "was a peasant who worked on the land (*homo rusticus laborator et cultivator terre*), a disorderly person who frequented taverns and gambling places and was of base condition." Moreover, Giovanni and his brothers were usurers, whose wealth derived from illegal banking operations. As proof of this allegation, the procurator asserted that Giovanni's house had once been daubed with red paint, "as was customarily done to the homes of manifest usurers and Jews in the city of Florence." One of Giovanni's own witnesses, Cipriano Nuti, admitted that he had heard this report. Such acts of popular censure are not well documented, though they may have been common. Was the gesture of spilling blood on the doorway of Cosimo de' Medici's new palace on the Via Larga similarly motivated by a desire to brand the Medici publicly as usurers and profiteers?

The insinuation of usury touched a sensitive

nerve among Florentine businessmen whose activities—and particularly their borrowing, lending and exchange of money—were often perceived as violations of the church's prohibitions against usury. Antoninus's court was the scene of numerous prosecutions against suspected usurers. Vespasiano da Bisticci wrote that Cosimo de' Medici "had prickings of conscience that certain portions of his wealth . . . had not been righteously gained," and he asked the advice of Pope Eugenius IV, who suggested that he build a monastery "if he was bent on unburdening his soul." Several of Giovanni's witnesses were questioned about the accusation of usury; their responses were cautiously neutral. Niccolò Magaldi stated that he had never heard any complaints about Giovanni's business practices. The Della Casa brothers, Giovanni Panciatichi testified, had obtained their wealth "in the same way as other merchants had done." Carlo Guasconi corroborated his opinion, stating that Giovanni's wealth had been accumulated "in the manner of merchants today (*more modernorum mercatorum*)," which might suggest that the standards of Florentine business ethics were more relaxed than in the past. Still, the notion that banking and moneylending were disreputable persisted in this community whose wealth and prosperity, to a substantial degree, were derived from such operations.

Wealth and its derivation was one criterion for measuring a family's reputation and thus its place in the complex and vaguely defined hierarchy of

social rank. The evaluation of fluctuating reputations was a major preoccupation of Florentine
parents responsible for arranging marriages for
their children. In these operations the marriage
market was not unlike a modern stock exchange;
indeed, marriageable girls were sometimes characterized as "merchandise" (*mercatanzia*). The
operations of the market are revealed in rich detail
in the correspondence of Alessandra Strozzi, a
Florentine widow who was actively engaged for
more than two decades, from 1447 to 1471, in
finding spouses for her daughters Caterina and
Alessandra and her sons Filippo and Lorenzo,
who were then living in Naples. A letter written
by her son-in-law Marco Parenti to Filippo
Strozzi in July 1465 graphically describes aspects
of that enterprise. Marco had investigated the
qualifications of two girls from the Adimari and
Tanagli families as prospective brides for Filippo;
he concluded that they were the best candidates
in the current market. Their dowries were of
equal size; their physical appearance was similar.
Marco conceded that the Adimari were more
"noble" than the Tanagli, but that advantage was
neutralized by the fact that the Adimari girl was
an orphan with no brothers, and her close relatives (uncles and cousins) were undistinguished
men. Though the Tanagli lineage did not rank so
high in the social order as the Adimari, "they are
old and worthy, and this branch is descended
from knights." Marco described the father of the
Tanagli girl as respectable, well-bred, and elo-
quent. He noted the prominent families linked to

the Tanagli by marriage: Alessandri, Guidetti, Ri-
dolfi, Vettori. "So that," Marco concluded, "bal-
ancing one and the other, there is not much difference, and we leave it to your judgment." In the
end Filippo Strozzi married neither girl, and Marco's efforts on his behalf were wasted.

The time and energy invested in these negotiations attest to the aristocracy's concern with
status that, by the mid-fifteenth century, may
have been more intense than in the past as a result
of sharper social distinctions, rising dowries, and
a consequent reduction of the number of eligibles
in the marriage market. Florence's elite was engaged in a process of self-definition, identifying
the social qualities that denoted honor and respectability and excluding those people whose
backgrounds did not qualify as "noble." Lusanna's efforts to breach that social barrier through
marriage would inevitably arouse resistance and
opposition not only from Giovanni della Casa's
family but from the ranks of the elite. The
evidence from marriage contracts and private
records supports the conclusion that the over-
whelming majority of Florentines chose their
marriage partners from their social equals. The
rare exceptions involved women of good family
marrying men of lesser status: for example, a
Lanfredini woman who had married a cloth
mender, and a Strozzi lady whose husband sold
wine at retail. No concrete evidence has yet been
found to substantiate the assertion by Lusanna's
procurator that in Florence "a woman's beauty
has often been the cause of marriages between

socially disparate partners, in which no dowry has been given." The state's disapproval of such mésalliances was illustrated by an edict of the Signoria in April 1500 that condemned a clandestine marriage between one Francesco of Cortona and a girl from his district. The Signoria did not seek to annul the marriage but imposed a jail sentence of six months on Francesco and ordered him to arrange a peace pact with the girl's godparents. In levying this penalty, the Signoria stated that "marriages in Florence and its territory should be public and not secret, contracted at proper times, and according to the customs of each place and the status of the spouses."

EPILOGUE

The testimony of the thirty witnesses in this case reveals a consensus about the nature of Florence's social order: a hierarchy with rough gradations of rank and status. Less clearly defined were the conventions that established standards of behavior and penalties for violations of those norms. By insisting upon the legitimacy of her marriage to Giovanni, Lusanna was challenging a basic tenet of the social order. As a member of the city's ruling elite, Giovanni had greater access to power than did Lusanna. She pursued and won her case against him in the archiepiscopal court, but he was able to make his influence felt in Rome. To grasp the political implications of the case, which are not fully revealed in its dossier, one must understand the nature of power in Medicean Florence, its exercise, and its limits.

Cosimo de' Medici did not rule Florence in the sense that a despot like Borso d'Este ruled Ferrara. He was certainly the most prominent and influential citizen in the regime, and his supporters controlled the important magistracies. But his authority was never absolute or total. His influence was exercised through an elaborate patronage network that linked him to members of his party. Through this complex, unofficial system, Cosimo dispensed favors to his allies, clients, and "creatures" in the form of offices, loans, remission of taxes, cancellation or reduction of judicial penalties, and letters of recommendation. Though not invented by the Medici, this system became more efficient and broader in scope under their aegis, embracing the entire city and the territory beyond its walls that was under Florentine control. At its outermost limits were Medici contacts in Rome, Milan, Naples, and Venice, utilized on behalf of friends and clients. Literally thousands of petitions to Cosimo requesting his aid exist in the voluminous correspondence of the Medici preserved in Florence's Archivio di Stato. These appeals were drafted by Florentines rich and poor, prominent and obscure; by residents of other towns and districts in the dominion; and by foreigners. The language of the letters suggests the complex nature of these patron–client bonds. "Never have I wished for anything more in life than to take shelter under the wing of your power and authority," wrote a poor artisan to Cosimo in 1434. From a higher niche in the social hierarchy, the aristocrat Giovanni Capponi explained to Cosimo's grandson Lorenzo that the Medici reputation "has been the reason why, in my and our house's needs, we have with assurance had recourse to you and to your ancestors, by whom graciously we have been exalted." In a letter to the heads of the Sienese government written in 1476, Lorenzo apologized for importuning them daily on behalf of petitioners, particularly in cases like this when "the wife, the father, and the relatives" of an accused criminal had asked him to intercede on their kinsman's behalf.

Giovanni della Casa and his brothers Antonio and Ruggiero were linked to the Medici by ties of economic interest, physical proximity, and political allegiance. They had all been employed in the Medici bank, and after establishing their independent companies, they continued to transact business with Medici companies in Florence, Rome, and Geneva. Like their San Lorenzo neighbors, the Ginori and the Pucci, the Della Casa were parvenus whose entrée into the Florentine ruling elite was quite recent. They had profited economically and politically from their Medici connections, and they would have turned automatically to Cosimo for assistance in this moment of need. They could also exploit their own network of friendships within the elite to procure witnesses (Gondi, Guasconi, Panciatichi) and lawyers (Guasconi, Accolti) who would support Giovanni in the lawsuit. Through the marriage connection with Piero di Cardinale Rucellai, the Della Casa had gained a powerful ally and Medicean supporter, who had been influential in arranging for Cosimo's return from exile in 1434. Unfortunately, no documents have survived to reveal the workings of this network, which indeed often functioned through oral rather than written communication.

Living, as she did, in a neighborhood filled with Medici—and Della Casa—partisans, Lusanna could not rely upon a comparable group of supporters to promote and defend her interests. Still, she must have had friends in addition to her family who used their connections and influence on her behalf in Rome and Florence. How otherwise to explain the letter sent by Pope Calixtus III to Antoninus instructing him to investigate Lusanna's complaint against Giovanni? It is possible that Lusanna's case was used by Medici opponents to embarrass Cosimo and his faction just three years before a major challenge to his authority by a group of upper-class dissidents. This hypothesis, if correct, would explain the decision of the Signoria to quash the charge of poisoning brought against Lusanna after she initiated her lawsuit in Antoninus's court. Not a scintilla of evidence exists to document these political machinations, if indeed they occurred. Lusanna obtained her most significant support from Archbishop Antoninus, who defended her valiantly against the *podestà* and ultimately decided that her cause was just. No one in Florence was less afraid of Cosimo or more willing to resist his efforts (if deemed improper) on behalf of friends. Antoninus stated his position eloquently in a letter to Cosimo's son Giovanni, who had petitioned him on behalf of a friend accused of occupying illegally a baptismal church. Refusing to absolve the Medici client from his excommunication, the archbishop wrote, "You are powerful citizens, and the church supports the small and the weak."

On 4 November 1455 Jacopo della Casa appeared before Antoninus's tribunal as procurator

A Renaissance scholar

for Giovanni, to appeal the archbishop's judgment concerning the legality of the marriage between his brother and Lusanna. "Perceiving myself and Giovanni to be grievously harmed" by that decision, Jacopo appealed the case to Pope Calixtus III. A notarial document dated 30 December 1455 indicated that the appeal had been transferred to Rome, where it was pending before a court (probably the Apostolic Rota) in the curia. The document referred to an accusation of usury against the Della Casa brothers that had previously been submitted to the archiepiscopal tribunal but that had also been moved to Rome for judgment. Since the Della Casa, like the Medici, had long been established in Rome, they were knowledgeable about the operations of the curial bureaucracy. They or their agents were intimately acquainted with the officials—cardinals, judges, notaries—who decided cases of disputed marriages. If necessary, they could ask for help from friends and associates in Rome and Florence, most obviously and most significantly from Cosimo de' Medici. The extant sources (Medici correspondence; diplomatic records; memoirs) contain no references to this case, which must have preoccupied not only the Della Casa and the Rucellai but also their friends. If Cosimo himself had been asked to intercede with his Rome contacts, he might have written or dictated a note to an influential cardinal or to his partner in the Rome bank, requesting that Giovanni's case receive a sympathetic hearing in the Rota. Cosimo had done as much—and more—for other friends.

On 16 June 1456, six months after Jacopo appeared before Antoninus to appeal his decision, he returned with a papal letter which the notary Ser Baldovino Baldovini certified but unfortunately did not copy in his protocol. Jacopo petitioned Antoninus to carry out the papal instructions, which apparently ruled that the marriage between Giovanni and Lusanna was null and void. The same letter was submitted to the officials in charge of the grain supply, nullifying the fine that had been levied against Giovanni. Though no copy of Calixtus's *breve* has yet been found in Florence or Rome, Giovanni's tax return of 1458 supports the conclusion that the pope had decided to nullify the marriage. Listed among Giovanni's dependents were his wife, Marietta, aged eighteen, and the slave girl Caterina, whom Giovanni had apparently taken from Lusanna. The papal reversal of Antoninus's judgment could be explained in terms of power, influence, and money applied effectively in the Roman curia by men who were experienced in these machinations. But assuming that the judges in the Rota were honest and conscientious officials who studied the case carefully, they could have found sufficient evidence to conclude that the marriage between Giovanni and Lusanna was not canonically valid and that Antoninus's decision was wrong in fact and in law.

For Giovanni della Casa, Lusanna's plaint in the archbishop's court and its aftermath in the Roman curia were distracting and expensive, but not ruinous, episodes in his career. His tax declaration of 1458 revealed that he and his brother Jacopo owned real estate valued at 2,000 florins and business investments of nearly 4,000 florins. When that report was submitted to the tax officials, Giovanni was in London seeking to retrieve money that had been owed to his dead brother Antonio. A decade later, in 1469, Giovanni's estate was valued at only 2,270 florins. As dependents he listed his thirty-year-old wife, Marietta; two nieces, the daughters of his brother Antonio; and three sons: Carlo, illegitimate, seventeen; Antonio, ten; and Pandolfo, eight years old. In his statement to the tax authorities, Giovanni stated that he was heavily in debt and had been forced to write off several business investments as failures. Two years earlier, in 1467, he had been imprisoned in Florence for failing to repay 4,000 florins that he owed to the cardinal of Rouen. His business affairs did not prosper in the 1470s, a difficult time for Florentine merchants and bankers. In 1478 Giovanni was excommunicated, either for engaging in usury or for defaulting on a debt to a cleric. Despite these misfortunes, which must have troubled his last years, Giovanni continued his business activities in Geneva and Rome. After his death in 1480, his son Pandolfo assumed control of the Rome company, which survived under Della Casa management until 1543. His widow, Marietta, died in 1511.

The vicissitudes of Giovanni della Casa's life can be sketched from the evidence in notarial and tax records, but no trace of Lusanna has been found in archival sources for the years after 1456.

She was not identified as a member of her brother Antonio's household in 1458; in his *catasto* declaration, he listed only himself, his wife, Cosa, and two children, Francesco and Lionarda. Nor does Lusanna appear as a widow or a married woman in the city's tax registers. Her name is not recorded in the *libri dei morti*, the "books of the dead," that identified those who died within the city walls. What was her fate after the invalidation of her marriage to Giovanni? Many Florentine widows chose to enter a convent as a boarder or to join one of the tertiary religious houses where, without taking vows, they could live together in a community and perform charitable services. But Lusanna does not appear to have been temperamentally suited for such a life. It is more likely that she remarried, perhaps to a resident of a town or village outside Florence who did not know or care about her past. The record of that marriage may still survive in the protocols of a notary. Some assiduous scholar may discover the contract or possibly Lusanna's testament with stipulations about her burial site and the disposition of her property. At some future date an addendum to this tale of love and marriage in Renaissance Florence may yet appear in the historical record.

Lusanna's last years are cloaked in obscurity, but for a brief moment in her life she achieved celebrity status. Her case attracted the attention of the city's establishment: the archbishop, the *podestà*, the Signoria, and leading figures of the Medicean party, including almost certainly Cosimo himself. One must admire the courage which impelled her to challenge Florence's social and political order, with its elaborate mechanisms designed to control and discipline members of her sex and class. Despite her initial victory in Antoninus's court, she was ultimately defeated by her adversaries. She paid a price in money and reputation for her temerity. Lusanna was a woman whose determination to fight for her rights has provided us, five hundred years later, with an opportunity to understand better the universe that she inhabited.

REFERENCES

Notarial Sources

The primary material for this story survives in Florence's Archivio di Stato: the notarial protocols of Ser Filippo Mazzei, which contain the transcript of the litigation in the archiepiscopal court; and the *catasto* records (1427–1478), which provide information about Florentine households—identity and age of individuals, property holdings, debts and credits.

Chronologically, the first document in this case is the record of Antoninus's interrogation of Fra Felice Asini on 15 May 1455. It is recorded in *Notarile ante-cosimiano* (hereafter *NA*), M 344 (1455–1479), fol. 12r–12v. Pope Calixtus III's letter to Antoninus instructing him to investigate Lusanna's allegations is copied in *NA*, M 343 (1445–1450), fol. 175r–175v. The archbishop's acceptance of the letter and the nomination of procurators are in ibid., fol. 176v–178v. The initial deposition of Lusanna's procurator (14 July 1455) is in another volume redacted by Mazzei: *NA*, M 342 (1439–1482), fol. 103r–104v. The deposition of Giovanni's procurator is in *NA*, M 342 (1445–1450), fol. 202r–204v. The interrogation of witnesses called on Lusanna's behalf is in *NA*, M 342 (1439–1482), fol. 143r–161v: the testimony of Cosa, Lusanna's sister-in-law (143r–146v); Mea, her mother-in-law (147r–150r);

her brother Antonio (153r–155v); Fra Felice Asini (150v–153v); the servant Ammannato (156r–156v); and the peasants from Pitiana (157v–161v). The testimony of Giovanni's witnesses is in *NA*, M 342 (1439–1482), fol. 106r–142v, 180r–187v. The most important witnesses are Fiora (106v–109v); Tita (110r–112r); Giuliana Magaldi (119r–122v); Niccolò Magaldi (124r–126r); Andrea Magaldi (127v–130r); Giovanni Panciatichi (131r–134r); Giuliano Gondi (134v–136r); Mazza del Mazza (137r–137v); Cipriano Nuti (138r–139r); Piero Cavicciuli (140v–142r); Antonio, Giovanni's servant (142r–142v, 180r); Carlo Guasconi (182v); Bartolomeo Magaldi (185r–186r).

The record of court proceedings from 3 June 1455 until the pronouncement of the sentence in favor of Lusanna on 29 October 1455 is in *NA*, M 343 (1445–1450), fol. 179r–259v. The documents pertaining to Antoninus's quarrel with the *podestà* are in ibid., fol. 183r–189r; Antoninus's sentence: *NA*, M 343 (1445–1450), fol. 257r–259v; the protest against that sentence by Giovanni's procurator: ibid., fol. 260r–260v; later references to Giovanni's appeal to Rome: *NA*, I 34 (1450–1455), unpaginated, 10 November 1455, 30 December 1455; the reference to the papal letter to Antoninus reversing his decision: *NA*, B 382 (1439–1464), fol. 197r–197v (16 June 1456).

Catasto Reports

The 1430 and 1433 *catasto* declarations of Maestro Benedetto di Girolamo are in *Catasto*, 382, fol. 770r–773v; 498, fol. 98v–99v. The 1430 returns of Antonio Nucci, the father of Lusanna's first husband, and of

Giovanni's father, Ser Lodovico della Casa: *Catasto*, 407, fol. 188r–188v, 350r–351v. The 1458 return of Giovanni and Jacopo della Casa: *Catasto*, 822, fol. 491v–507v; Giovanni's 1469 report: ibid., 923, fol. 916r–918v. In 1427 Antoninus's mother, Monna Sandra, "donna fu de ser Niccolò Pierozzi," owned a house in the Via del Cocomero, where she lived with a servant girl: *Catasto*, 55, fol. 325r.

1. The Context

The history of the Della Casa lineage has been recently described by Michele Cassandro in the preface to his edition of the account book of the company headed by Antonio di Ser Lodovico della Casa: *Il libro giallo di Ginevra della compagnia fiorentina di Antonio della Casa e Simone Guadagni* (Prato, 1976). A genealogical history of the Rucellai was compiled by Luigi Passerini, *Genealogia e storia della famiglia Rucellai* (Florence, 1861). A more recent and more sophisticated study is Francis William Kent, *Household and Lineage in Renaissance Florence: The Family Life of the Capponi, Ginori, and Rucellai* (Princeton, 1977). Kent has also dedicated a monograph to Giovanni Rucellai, the most notable member of that lineage in the fifteenth century, in *Giovanni Rucellai ed il suo zibaldone*, vol. 2, *A Florentine Patrician and His Palace* (London, 1981). Obscure artisan families like those of Maestro Benedetto di Girolamo and his son-in-law Andrea di Antonio Nucci have not attracted biographers and have received only sporadic attention from historians. Richard Goldthwaite has written about the craftsmen and laborers in the building trades, who were roughly comparable professionally and socially to tailors and bakers: *The Building of Renaissance Florence* (Baltimore and London, 1980), 242–35.

The major biography of Archbishop Antoninus is Raoul Morçay, *Saint Antonin fondateur du couvent du Saint-Marc archevêque de Florence (1389–1459)* (Paris and Tours, 1914). More recent studies include Stefano Orlandi, *S. Antonino* (Florence, 1959); and Carlo Calzolai, *Frate Antonino Pierozzi dei Domenicani, arcivescovo di Firenze* (Rome, 1961). David Peterson's doctoral dissertation is an important contribution to the scholarship on Antoninus: "Archbishop Antoninus: Florence and the Church in the Earlier Fifteenth Century" (Cornell University, 1984). Vespasiano da Bisticci's biographical sketch has been translated: *Renaissance Princes, Popes and Prelates. The Vespasiano Memoirs: Lives of Illustrious Men of the XVth Century* (New York: Harper Torchbooks, 1963), 157–63. Pope Calixtus III and his pontificate are described by Michael Mallett in *The Borgias* (London, 1969), ch. 4.

II. The History of a Relationship

Marriage

The ambiguities surrounding the institution of marriage in Europe prior to the Council of Trent are neatly summarized by Erwin Panofsky, "Jan van Eyck's Arnolfini Portrait," printed in *Renaissance Art*, ed. Creighton Gilbert (New York: Harper Torchbooks, 1970), 6–7: "Although the Church did its very best to caution the faithful against marrying secretly, there was no proper 'impedimentum clandestinitatis' until 1563; that is to say, two people could contract a perfectly valid and legitimate marriage whenever and wherever they liked, without any witness and independently of any ecclesiastical rite, provided that the essential condition of a 'mutual consent expressed by words and action' had been fulfilled."

Marriage customs in Italy during the Renaissance are described in two older works: Francesco Brandileone, *Saggi sulla storia della celebrazione del matrimonio in Italia* (Milan, 1906); and Nino Tamassia, *La famiglia italiana nei secoli decimoquinto e decimosesto* (Milan, 1910). Two recent studies with rich bibliography are Brucia Witthoft, "Marriage Rituals," *Artibus et historiae*, no. 5 (1982): 43–59; and Christiane Klapisch-Zuber, "Zacharias; or The Ousting of the Father: The Rites of Marriage in Tuscany from Giotto to the Council of Trent," in *Ritual, Religion, and the Sacred: Selections from the* Annales, économies, sociétés, civilisations, vol. 7, ed. Robert Forster and Orest Ranum, trans. Elsbeth Forster and Patricia Ranum (Baltimore and London, 1982), 24–56. Klapisch-Zuber, in collaboration with David Herlihy, has also written on Tuscan marriage in *Les Toscans et leurs familles* (Paris, 1978), 393–419, 585–606. Samuel Cohn has analyzed patrician and "lower-class" marriages in *The Laboring Classes in Renaissance Florence* (New York, 1980). Some legal issues in marriage are described by Thomas Kuehn, "Women, Marriage and *Patria Potestas* in Late Medieval Florence," *Tijdschrift voor Rechtsgeschiedenis*, 49 (1981): 127–47.

On the critical issue of dowries, two recent articles have been published as preliminary studies of a larger work: Julius Kirshner, "Pursuing Honor While Avoiding Sin: The *Monte delle Doti* of Florence," *Studi senesi*, 89 (1977): 177–258; and Julius Kirshner and Anthony Molho, "The Dowry Fund and the Marriage

Market in Early Quattrocento Florence," *Journal of Modern History*, 50 (1978): 403–38. See, too, Christiane Klapisch-Zuber, "Le complexe de Griselda: Dot et dons de mariage au Quattrocento," *Mélanges de l'Ecole française de Rome (moyen âge, temps modernes*, 94 (1982): 7–44.

Marriage Separations, Annulments, Dissolutions

The major study in English on this rich and relatively unexplored topic is John Noonan, *Power to Dissolve* (Cambridge, Mass., 1972), which focuses upon the subject in the context of canon law. Two important regional studies are Richard Helmholz, *Marriage Litigation in Medieval England* (Cambridge, 1974); and Thomas Safley, *Let No Man Put Asunder: The Control of Marriage in the German Southwest* (Kirksville, Mo., 1984). I am not aware of any scholarly study of the dissolution of marriage in medieval and Renaissance Florence.

Florentine archival references to petitions for dissolution of marriage after consummation: *NA*, M 347 (1426–1450), unpaginated, no. 8, August 1427 (Taddea di Antonio de Rencine); ibid., unpaginated, no. 25, 24 September 1429 (Antonia di Tommaso Ferretti); *NA*, F 507 (1427–1430), fol. 154r–155r, 16 July 1429 (Maria di Oliviero de Burgo); *NA*, I 33 (1440–1444), unpaginated, 7 September 1443 (Alessandra di Piero Gollini); *NA*, D 88 (1458–1461), fol. 354r–355v, 11 December 1461 (Francesca di Ser Giovanni Arnoldi); *NA*, D 89 (1466–1469), fol. 76r, 2 January 1467 (Tessa di Bartolomeo della Zecca). Petitions of wives for legal separation: *NA*, T 93, unpaginated, 25 August 1442 (Antonia di Cecco Angeli of Firenzuola); *NA*, P

128 (1452–1462), fol. 416v–417r, 18 November 1460 (Appollonia di Domenico Lulli); *NA*, M 570 (1461–1467), fol. 163r–164v (Alessandra di Ubertino de' Bardi). Petitions to break promises of marriage (*sponsalia*) prior to consummation: *NA*, A 279, fol. 226r, 14 September 1458 (Brigida di Antonio Giovanni of La Spezia); *NA*, M 571, fol. 59r, 22 December 1473 (Margherita di Giovanni of San Casciano); ibid., fol. 218v, 23 October 1475 (Marina di Francesco de Raugia); ibid., fol. 301r–301v, 14 August 1476 (Pippa di Giovanni di Piero); *NA*, D 93 (1489–1490), fol. 2v–3v, 19 April 1490 (Marietta di Ser Guaspare di Simone); *NA*, D 94 (1491), fol. 11r, 15 April 1491 (Caterina di Meo).

III. The Quest for Justice

Sources

The record of the proceedings in this case is described above, under the rubric "Notarial Sources." The Signoria's order to the *podestà* to cease his investigation of Lusanna is recorded in *Signori e collegi, deliberazioni (ordinaria autorità)*, 79, fol. 4v, 4 September 1455. Antoninus discussed marriage and its legal aspects in his *Summa theologica* (Verona, 1740; reprint Graz, 1959), book 3, title 1, cap. 1–23. The case of Berta is cited in cap. 8, clandestine marriages in cap. 16, *sponsalia* in cap. 18. The archbishop's description of canon law procedures and problems is in ibid., book 3, title 9, cap. 1–16; and, specifically, witnesses and their credibility in cap. 11. The early constitutions of the Florentine episcopate have been edited by Richard Trexler, *Synodal Law in Florence and Fiesole, 1306–1518*

(Vatican City, 1971); Antoninus's comments on marriage, ibid., 124–25. There is corroboration of the charge that Fra Felice Asini was convicted of a crime in a Cortona court; the official who imposed the sentence was excommunicated for violating the friar's ecclesiastical immunity: Archivio Segreto Vaticano (hereafter ASV), *Archivio della Sacra Penitenziaria*, 5, fol. 54v, 4 June 1455. Giuliana Magaldi's partial retraction of her testimony is in *NA*, M 343 (1447–1459), fol. 78r, 7 October 1455. The evidence of suborned witnesses in Feltre is in Gigi Corazol and Loredana Corrà, eds., *Esperimenti d'amore: Fatti di giovani nel Veneto del Cinquecento* (Vicenza, 1981), 26, 74, 125, 141. The 1457 case involving a marriage between two adulterers from the diocese of Lucerne is described in ASV, *Archivio della Sacra Penitenziaria*, 5, fol. 321r–321v, 13 February 1454. Similar cases are noted in ibid., 3, fol. 59r, 266r–266v; 5, 289v–290r, 332v. The Signoria's statement about Antoninus's "persecution" of accused usurers is in *Signori, carteggi, legazioni e commissarie*, 13, fol. 46r, 23 November 1453. Antoninus's self-description as *pater pauperum et miserabilium personarum* is in *NA*, M 343 (1443–1454), fol. 103r, 4 October 1451.

Judicial Process

The standard work on canon law procedure is Ludwig Wahrmund, *Quellen zur Geschichte des römisch-canonischen Processes im Mittelalter*, 5 vols. (Innsbruck, 1905–31). Lauro Martines has written a valuable study on Florentine civil and canon lawyers: *Lawyers and Statecraft in Renaissance Florence* (Princeton, 1968). Richard Trexler discusses the functioning of the episcopal court in *Synodal Law in Florence and Fiesole,*

1306–1518 (Vatican City, 1971), 136–72. A recent and
informative study of Florentine legal theory and practice: Thomas Kuehn, *Emancipation in Late Medieval
Florence* (New Brunswick, N.J., 1982).

IV. Love, Marriage, and the Social Order

Sexuality and Women's Roles

A useful introduction to this problem is Julia
O'Faolain and Lauro Martines, *Not in God's Image*
(London, 1973). A recent and instructive study on
Venice: Guido Ruggiero, *The Boundaries of Eros: Sex
Crime and Sexuality in Renaissance Venice* (New York,
1985). Much of the Florentine evidence derives from
literary works (e.g., Boccaccio's *Decameron*; Gentile
Sermini's *Novelle*) and from sermons (e.g., San Ber-
nardino of Siena; Savonarola). Private correspondence and family memoirs, or *ricordanze*, also contain
information on these topics, almost wholly from a
masculine perspective. A comprehensive bibliography appears in David Herlihy and Christiane Klapisch-Zuber, *Les Toscans et leurs familles* (Paris, 1978),
665–70. Extremely rare are documents penned by
Florentine women. They include the letters of Alessandra Strozzi, *Lettere di un gentildonna fiorentina del secolo XV ai figliuoli esuli*, ed. Cesare Guasti (Florence,
1877); those of Margherita Datini, cited in Iris Origo,
The Merchant of Prato (New York, 1957); and female
members of the Medici family in Janet Ross, *Lives of
the Early Medici as Told in Their Correspondence* (London, 1910), and Yvonne Macguire, *The Women of the
Medici* (London, 1927). An idealized biography of
Alessandra de' Bardi was written by Vespasiano da

Bisticci: *Renaissance Princes, Popes, and Prelates. The Vespasiano Memoirs: Lives of Illustrious Men of the XVth Century* (New York: Harper Torchbooks, 1963), 439–62; a "model" housewife was described by Leonbattista Alberti in *The Family in Renaissance Florence*, tr. Renée N. Watkins (Columbia, S.C., 1969), 206–15.

The secondary literature on Florentine women and their roles is thin: Janet Ross, "The Middle-Class Child in Urban Italy, Fourteenth to Early Sixteenth Century," in *The History of Childhood*, ed. Lloyd deMause (New York, 1974), 182–228; Lauro Martines, "Looking at Women in Renaissance Florence," *Journal of Medieval and Renaissance Studies*, 4 (1974): 15–28; Judith Brown, "A Woman's Place Was in the Home: Women's Work in Renaissance Tuscany," in *Rewriting the Renaissance: The Discourses of Sexual Difference in Early Modern Europe*, ed. Marjorie Ferguson, Maureen Quilligan, and Nancy Vickers (Chicago, 1984); Christiane Klapisch-Zuber, "La 'mère cruelle': Maternité, veuvage et dot dans la Florence des XIVᵉ-XVᵉ siècles," *Annales*, 38 (1983): 1097–1109; Richard Trexler, "La prostitution florentine au XVᵉ siècle: Patronages et clientèles," *Annales*, 36 (1981): 983–1015; Thomas Kuehn, "*Cum consensu mundualdi*: Legal Guardianship of Women in Quattrocento Florence," *Viator*, 13 (1982): 309–33; Francis William Kent, "A Proposal by Savonarola for the Self-Reform of Florentine Women (March 1496)," *Memorie Domenicane*, new ser., 14 (1983): 335–41.

Family

The literature on the Florentine Renaissance family is extensive. The works cited above on marriage and on women's roles discuss many aspects of the family.

A recent and important analysis: Francis William Kent, *Household and Lineage in Renaissance Florence: The Family Life of the Capponi, Ginori, and Rucellai* (Princeton, 1977). Florentine memoirs are a rich source of information on the family. An inventory of surviving *ricordanze* has now been compiled: Fulvio Pezzarossa, "La tradizione fiorentina della memorialistica. Con un'appendice: Per un catalogo dei testi memorialistici fiorentiana a stampa," in Gian Maria Anselmi et al., *La "memoria" dei mercatores* (Bologna, 1980).

Neighborhood

The social structure of Florentine neighborhoods has been discussed by Samuel Cohn, *The Laboring Classes in Renaissance Florence* (New York, 1980); and by Francis William Kent and Dale Kent, *Neighbours and Neighbourhood in Renaissance Florence: The District of the Red Lion in the Fifteenth Century* (Locust Valley, N.Y., 1982). The Kents have pursued their exploration of this subject in "Two Vignettes of Florentine Society in the Fifteenth Century," *Rinascimento*, 23 (1983): 237–60. Francis William Kent has published another article on this topic: "Il ceto dirigente fiorentino e i vincoli di 'vicinanza' nel Quattrocento," in *Atti del VI Convegno sul ceto dirigente in Toscana* (Florence, 1984).

"Class" Prejudice and Hostility

Class divisions and enmities as a fundamental dimension of Florentine social history in the Renaissance have been emphasized most forcefully by Samuel Cohn, *The Laboring Classes in Renaissance Florence*

(New York, 1980); and by Anthony Molho, "Cosimo de' Medici: *Pater Patriae* or Padrino?" *Stanford Italian Review*, 1 (1979): 5–33, and "Italian History in American Universities," in *Italia e Stati Uniti d'America: concordanze e dissonanze* (Rome, 1981), 201–44.

Mercantile Ethics and Usury

Two Italian scholars, Armando Sapori and Federigo Melis, and a Belgian-American historian, Raymond de Roover, have explored most assiduously the *mentalité* of Florentine businessmen. Sapori's views are summarized in *The Italian Merchant in the Middle Ages* (New York, 1970), and in his collection of articles, *Studi di storia economica* (secoli XIII–XIV–XV), 2 vols. (Florence, 1955). Melis's masterwork is a biography of Francesco Datini: *Aspetti della vita economica medievale* (Siena, 1962). De Roover's major publications are collected in *The Rise and Decline of the Medici Bank 1397–1494* (Cambridge, Mass., 1963), and *Business, Banking, and Economic Thought in Late Medieval and Early Modern Europe*, ed. Julius Kirshner (Chicago, 1974). Benjamin Nelson has written the classic study of usury, *The Idea of Usury* (Princeton, 1949). Dale Kent discusses the defacement of the Medici palace in "The Importance of Being Eccentric: Giovanni Cavalcanti's View of Cosimo de' Medici's Florence," *Journal of Medieval and Renaissance Studies*, 9 (1979): 131.

Marriages Appropriate
and Inappropriate

Marco Parenti's letter to Filippo Strozzi (July 1465) is printed in *Lettere di una gentildonna fiorentina del secolo XV ai figliuoli esuli*, ed. Cesare Guasti (Florence, 1877),

449. Marriages between socially unequal partners are described in *NA*, P 128 (1439–1450), fol. 494r, 17 February 1451; and ibid., D 86 (1449–1455), unpaginated, 26 June 1453. The Signoria's penalization of Francesco da Cortona is recorded in *Signori e collegi, deliberazioni (ordinaria autorità)*, 102, fol. 95r–95v, 3 August 1500.

v. Epilogue

The letters illustrating patron–client relations are quoted in Dale Kent, *The Rise of the Medici: Faction in Florence 1426–1434* (Oxford, 1978), 86; Francis William Kent, *Household and Lineage in Renaissance Florence: The Family Life of the Capponi, Ginori, and Rucellai* (Princeton, 1977), 212; and Lorenzo de' Medici, *Lettere*, ed. N. Rubinstein (Florence, 1977–), vol. 2, no. 212. Piero di Cardinale Rucellai's close ties to the Medici are noted by Kent, *Household and Lineage*, 219. Archbishop Antoninus's letter concerning the excommunication of a Medici client is in *Mediceo avanti il principato*, VI, 208, 8 December 1456. I am grateful to Dale Kent for giving me this citation.

The references to Giovanni della Casa's appeal of his sentence to Rome are in *NA*, M 343 (1445–1450), fol. 260r–260v; ibid., I 34 (1450–1455), unpaginated, 1 November, 18 and 30 December 1455. Giovanni's tax declarations of 1458 and 1469 are in *Catasto*, 822, fol. 490r–502r; 925, fol. 100r–101r. His business difficulties that culminated in his imprisonment are mentioned in *NA*, G 617 (1466–1469), fol. 171r–173r; ibid., G 590 (1475–1479), fol. 165v.

SOURCES FOR ILLUSTRATIONS

The illustrations in this volume were
selected from various contemporary sources
depicting subject matter appropriate for the
story of Giovanni and Lusanna. The original
woodcuts have been touched up and enlarged
or reduced for reproduction.

JACKET FRONT: *Portrait of a Man and Woman at a
Casement*, by an unknown Florentine painter of the
mid–fifteenth century (the workshop of Filippo Lippi).
Courtesy of the Metropolitan Museum, New York.

JACKET BACK: From *Fior di Virtù*, Florence, 1491.

FRONTIS   From *Storia di Uberto e Filomena*, n.p.,
n.d.

PAGE 7   From Jacobus de Cessolis, *Libro di
giuocho di scacchi*, Miscomini edition, Florence, 1493.

PAGE 17   From Giovanni Boccaccio, *Decamerone*,
de Gregoriis edition, Venice, 1492.

PAGE 23   From Giovanni Boccaccio, *Decamerone*,
de Gregoriis edition, Venice, 1492.

PAGE 31   From Giovanni Boccaccio, *Ninfale
Fiesolano*, Panizzi edition, Florence, 1568.

PAGE 41   From *Novella di Gualtieri e Griselda*,
n.p., n.d.

PAGE 51   From Giovanni Boccaccio, *Decamerone*,
de Gregoriis edition, Venice, 1492.

PAGE 59   From *Storia di Maria per Ravenna*, n.p., n.d.

PAGE 67   From *Contrasto di carnesciale e la quaresima*, Florence, n.d.

PAGE 81   From Aesop, *Vita e fabulae*, Tuppo edition, Naples, 1485.

PAGE 87   From Giovanni Boccaccio, *Decamerone*, de Gregoriis edition, Venice, 1492.

PAGE 97   From *Contrasto di carnesciale e la quaresima*, Florence, n.d.

PAGE 103   From Masuccio Salernitano, *Novellino*, de Gregoriis edition, Venice, 1492.

PAGE 115   From Jacobus de Cessolis, *Libro di giuocho di scacchi*, Miscomini edition, Florence, 1493.

DESIGNER:	*Wolfgang Lederer*
COMPOSITOR:	*Wilsted & Taylor*
TEXT:	*11/13 Bembo*
DISPLAY:	*Bembo*
PRINTER:	*Vail-Ballou Press*
BINDER:	*Vail-Ballou Press*